BASIC

THIRD EDITION

READING POWER 1

Extensive Reading • Vocabulary Building • Comprehension Skills • Thinking Skills

Linda Jeffries

Beatrice S. Mikulecky

PEARSON
Longman

Basic Reading Power 1, Third Edition

Pearson Education, 10 Bank Street, White Plains, NY 10606

Staff credits: The people who made up the *Basic Reading Power 1, Third Edition* team, representing editorial, production, design, and manufacturing, are Pietro Alongi, Danielle Belfiore, John Brezinsky, Dave Dickey, Oliva Fernandez, Massimo Rubini, Barbara Sabella, Jaimie Scanlon, Jennifer Stem, Paula Van Ells, and Pat Wosczyk.

Text design and composition: Word & Image Design Studio, Inc.
Text font: 13.5/15 Caslon
Illustrations and tech art: Burgandy Beam and Word & Image Design Studio, Inc.
Credits: See page 229.

Library of Congress Cataloging-in-Publication Data
Mikulecky, Beatrice S.
    Reading power 1: extensive reading, vocabulary building, comprehension skills, thinking skills/Beatrice S. Mikulecky, Linda Jeffries.—3rd ed.
    p. cm.
    Rev. ed. of: Basic reading power, 2nd ed., 2004.
    ISBN 0-13-814389-7
    1. English language—Textbooks for foreign speakers. 2. Reading comprehension—Problems, exercises, etc. 3. Thought and thinking—Problems, exercises, etc. 4. Vocabulary—Problems, exercises, etc. I. Jeffries, Linda. II. Title. III. Title: Reading power one.
    PE1128.M565 2009
    428.6'4–dc22

                                                                    2009013788

ISBN-13: 978-0-13-814389-3
ISBN-10: 0-13-814389-7

Printed in the United States of America
1 2 3 4 5 6 7 8 9 10—DBH—13 12 11 10 09

Contents

Acknowledgments

I would like to thank teachers around the world for their feedback regarding *Basic Reading Power 1*. The following colleagues and reviewers have been particularly helpful: Anna Masetti, University of Modena; Anna Feldman Leibovich, Ph.D, Forest Hills High School, Forest Hills, NY; Deirdre Garr, Oxon Hill Middle School, Fort Washington, MD; and Laura Leek, Sacramento City College, Sacramento, CA.

I am also very much indebted to the development editor, Jaimie Scanlon, who helped me enormously with her sharp eye for detail and her clear vision of the book as a whole, as well as with her patience and sense of humor.

Thanks,
Linda

About the Authors

Linda Jeffries holds a master's degree in TESOL from Boston University. She has taught reading, writing and ESL/EFL at Boston College, Boston University, the Harvard University Summer ESL Program, the University of Opole, Poland, and the University of Bologna, Italy. She lives in Italy, near Bologna, and teaches academic reading and writing at the University of Modena.

Bea Mikulecky holds a master's degree in TESOL and a doctorate in Applied Psycholinguistics from Boston University. In addition to teaching reading, writing, and ESL, she has worked as a teacher trainer in the Harvard University Summer ESL Program, in the Simmons College MATESL Program, and in Moscow, Russia. She is the author of *A Short Course in Teaching Reading Skills*.

Introduction to *Basic Reading Power 1*

To the Teacher

Basic Reading Power 1 is unlike most other reading textbooks. First, the book is organized in a different way. It has four separate parts that correspond to four important aspects of proficient reading, and therefore it is like four books in one. **Teachers should assign work on all four parts of the book concurrently.**

The four parts of *Basic Reading Power 1* are:

- Part 1: Extensive Reading
- Part 2: Vocabulary Building
- Part 3: Comprehension Skills
- Part 4: Thinking Skills

Second, the focus of *Basic Reading Power 1* is different. While most books focus on content, this book directs students' attention to their own reading processes. The aim is for students to develop a strategic approach to reading at this early stage, so that they learn to view reading in English as a problem-solving activity rather than a translation exercise. This will enable them to acquire good reading habits and skills, and to build confidence in their abilities, and thus help them gain access more quickly to English-language material for study, work, or pleasure.

For a successful outcome, teachers should follow the indications for work in pairs or small groups. Talking about their work will help students formulate ideas and consolidate vocabulary learning.

Basic Reading Power 1 is intended for students who are in a beginning-level English program. It is assumed that students who use this book will be literate and have an English vocabulary of about 300 words. They should be familiar with the simple present, present continuous, simple past, and future tenses.

In this third edition of *Basic Reading Power 1*, the approach remains the same as in the earlier editions, though in response to recent research as well as feedback from teachers, there is more emphasis on vocabulary acquisition and learning strategies. All the units have been updated and more guidance has been added for students in learning the skills. The major changes in this edition include:

Part 1: Extensive Reading—new fables and stories; more guidance in vocabulary learning

Part 2: Vocabulary Building—more guidance in vocabulary-learning methods including dictionary work and strategies for guessing meaning from context; more extensive work on word parts (prefixes, suffixes, and word families); focus on collocation and lexical phrases

Part 3: Comprehension Skills—a new "Focus on Vocabulary" section in each unit with a reading passage containing 10 target words and exercises to teach these words

Part 4: Thinking Skills—a gradual increase in difficulty of the items as students progress through the units; new items

A separate Teacher's Guide contains the answer key, a rationale for the approach taken in *Basic Reading Power 1*, specific suggestions for using it in the classroom, and a sample syllabus.

To the Student

Basic Reading Power 1 can help you learn to read well in English. In this book, you will work on reading in four ways in the four parts of the book:

- Part 1: Extensive Reading—reading a lot
- Part 2: Comprehension Skills—learning to understand what you read
- Part 3: Vocabulary Building—learning new words
- Part 4: Thinking Skills—learning to think in English

Work on **all four parts** of the book every week. You can learn to be a good reader in English!

Vocabulary in *Basic Reading Power 1*

The following activities introduce some of the words and types of exercises you will find in *Basic Reading Power 1*. Ask your teacher if you have any questions.

A. *These words are in the sentences on page vii. Do you know them? Read each word or phrase. Then put a ✓ (you know), ? (you aren't sure), or X (you don't know) before the word.*

_____ circle	_____ correctly	_____ through	_____ aloud
_____ underline	_____ belong	_____ check	_____ complete
_____ missing	_____ cross out	_____ pronunciation	_____ passage

B. Work with another student. Read and follow the directions in the sentences.

1. Circle the last word in this (sentence.)

2. Underline the first word in this sentence.

3. A word is missing from this _____. Write the word.

4. One word in this sentecne isn't spelled correctly. Write that word correctly: _____

5. One word in this sentence flowers doesn't belong. Cross out that word.

6. Some words are not easy to pronounce. Can you pronounce *through*?

7. Check your pronunciation with your teacher. Are you saying it correctly?

8. Practice saying *through* aloud.

9. Complete the passage with words from the box.

> watched   was   went

    Yesterday it rained all day. We didn't go for a walk. We _____ a soccer game on television. In the evening, we _____ to see a movie. It _____ very good. We liked it a lot.

10. Show your work to another pair of students. Did you answer the questions the same way?

C. Think again about the words on the list in part A. Write any new words on the list below. Then look them up in the dictionary and write the meanings. Check your work with your teacher.

Words	Meanings
_____	_____
_____	_____
_____	_____
_____	_____

PART

1

Extensive Reading

Introduction

What does reading mean to you?

A. Complete this questionnaire about reading in your life.

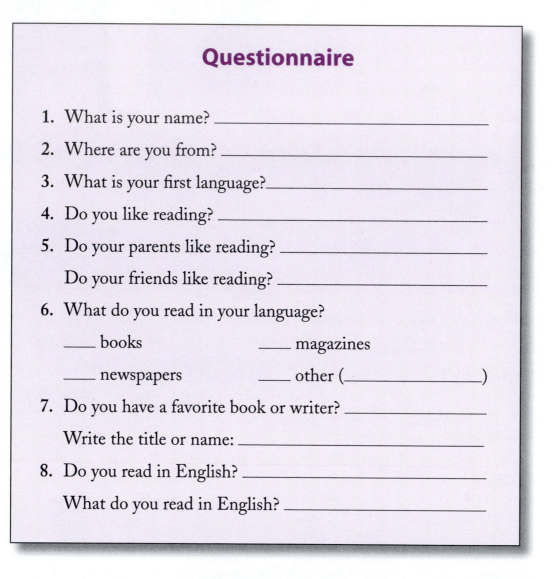

Questionnaire

1. What is your name? _____

2. Where are you from? _____

3. What is your first language?_____

4. Do you like reading? _____

5. Do your parents like reading? _____

    Do your friends like reading? _____

6. What do you read in your language?

    ____ books   ____ magazines

    ____ newspapers   ____ other (_____)

7. Do you have a favorite book or writer? _____

    Write the title or name: _____

8. Do you read in English? _____

    What do you read in English? _____

B. Talk about your answers with another student. Are they the same?

What Is Extensive Reading?

- reading a lot—many stories or books in a semester
- choosing what *you* want to read
- reading as fast or as slow as you want
- not having any tests on your reading

Why Is Extensive Reading Important?

Extensive reading will help you
... read faster.
... learn new words.
... write better.
... learn about the world.

When you read a lot, you see lots of words and sentences. You learn how they are used. You begin to think in English. But this only happens if you read *a lot*!

In Part 1, you will begin reading fables and stories. Then you will choose your own books.

New Vocabulary in Your Extensive Reading

Sometimes stories have words you don't know. Do you need to know all the words? No! You can understand the story without some words.

What should you do when you find new words?
- Read some more.
- Try to guess the meaning of the new word. (See Part 2, Unit 4, page 87.)
- Or try to understand the passage without the word. (See Exercise 1 on the next page.)
- Don't stop to look for every new word in the dictionary. This takes time, and sometimes you forget what you are reading.
- Look up the word only if you can't guess the meaning and it's important for the meaning of the passage.

Now practice reading passages with missing words. This is like reading a passage with words you don't know.

A. Read these paragraphs, but don't try to guess the missing words. Then answer the questions.

1. Magda is a student at Poznan University in Poland. She's 23 years old. She xxxxx in Mosina, a small xxxxx near the city of Poznan. Every xxxxx Magda takes the train to the city. She goes to her xxxxx at the university. After her classes, she studies with her friends at the xxxxx. In the evening, she sometimes has xxxxx with her friends at a restaurant. Then she takes the xxxxx home, and she studies some more. She wants to xxxxx a doctor. She must study hard for many xxxxx!

   a. Where does Magda live? _____

   b. What does she do in Poznan? _____

   c. What does she do in the evening? _____

   d. What is she studying? _____

2. Gerald is a student at Boston University in Boston, Massachusetts. He's 21 years old, and he's from a xxxxx town in California. He xxxxx in an apartment with other students. He's xxxxx Chinese language and history. Xxxxx year he is going to China. He xxxxx to learn Chinese well. When he's in China, he will also xxxxx all around the country. He wants to xxxxx Chinese people and see how they live. After he xxxxx his studies, Gerald would like to go into business. In the future, he would like to xxxxx for a company that buys and xxxxx things in China.

   a. Where is Gerald from? _____

   b. Where does he live? _____

   c. What is he studying? _____

   d. What does he want to do in the future? _____

B. Talk about your answers with another student. Are they the same?

Remember

You don't always need to know all the words. You can often understand the meaning of a passage with missing or new words.

EXERCISE 2

A. Read the paragraphs again. Now try to guess the missing words. Write the words in the blanks.

1. Magda is a student at Poznan University in Poland. She's 23 years old. She _____ in Mosina, a small _____ near the city of Poznan. Every _____ Magda takes the train to the city. She goes to her _____ at the university. After her classes, she studies with her friends at the _____. In the evening, she sometimes has _____ with her friends at a restaurant. Then she takes the _____ home, and she studies some more. She wants to _____ a doctor. She must study hard for many _____!

2. Gerald is a student at Boston University in Boston, Massachusetts. He's 21 years old, and he's from a _____ town in California. He _____ in an apartment with other students. He's _____ Chinese language and history. _____ year he is going to China. He _____ to learn Chinese well. When he's in China, he will also _____ all around the country. He wants to _____ Chinese people and see how they live. After he _____ his studies, Gerald would like to go into business. In the future, he would like to _____ for a company that buys and _____ things in China.

B. Talk about your answers with another student. Are they the same?

Remember

You can tell a lot about a word from the other words and sentences around it. You can often guess the meaning. You will practice this more in Part 2, Unit 4, page 87.

Note: For this class, you will need a notebook for new vocabulary. See Part 2, Unit 1, page 71 for how to use your vocabulary notebook.

UNIT 1

Fables

The fables in this unit come from different parts of the world. They tell stories about people or animals. Fables are not true stories. But every fable has a moral (lesson) about life.

Follow these steps when you read the fables:

1. **Preview the fable.**
   - Read the title and look at the picture (if there is one).
   - Look quickly through the fable.
   - What do you think the fable is about?

2. **Read the fable to the end.**
   - Don't stop to look up new words (words you don't know) in the dictionary.

3. **Read the fable again. Underline the new words (words you don't know).**
   - Write the new words below the fable.
   - Look them up in the dictionary. Write the meaning beside the word.

4. **Read the fable a third time. Then talk about these questions with another student.**
   - What and who is the fable about?
   - What is the moral?
   - Do you like the fable? Why or why not?
   - Is it like any other fable you have read? If so, explain.

5. **Write the new words and their meanings in your vocabulary notebook. (See Part 2, Unit 1, page 71.)**

Fable 1

A. **Preview the fable. (Follow the steps above.)**

B. **Read the fable to the end.**

The Lion and the Mouse

One day a lion was sleeping. A mouse ran over his face and woke him up. The lion was angry. He caught the mouse and said, "I'll eat you up. That will teach you not to wake up the king of the animals!"

But the mouse cried, "Please don't eat me. I didn't want to wake you up. I'm very sorry. Please let me go. You will be glad some day. If you do this for me, I will do something for you."

The lion laughed at the mouse. "A little animal like you? How can you help a big, strong animal like me?" But he also thought, "This mouse really is very small. He's too small for dinner. He's even too small for a snack." So he let the mouse go.

A few days later, some hunters came and caught the lion. They tied him to a tree with strong ropes. Then they left him and went to the village. They wanted to keep the lion and sell him to the zoo. But they needed more men.

The lion roared and roared. He was very angry, but he couldn't move. The mouse heard the roaring and ran to him.

"Now you will see what I can do for you," he said. Little by little, the mouse cut through the ropes with his teeth. Soon the lion was free.

(one of Aesop's Fables from Greece)

C. **Read the fable again and underline the new words. Then choose four new words you want to learn. Look them up and write them with their meanings.**

Words	Meanings
_____	_____
_____	_____
_____	_____
_____	_____

D. *Read the fable a third time. Then talk about it with another student. (See the questions on page 6.)*

E. *Write the new words and meanings from Exercise C in your vocabulary notebook.*

Fable 2

A. *Preview the fable.*

B. *Read the fable to the end.*

The Thief and the Hotelkeeper

Once there was a thief. He needed a place to sleep, so he stayed in a hotel. The next morning, he had no money to pay for the room. He looked around the hotel. What could he do?

Then he saw the hotelkeeper sitting just outside the door. He was wearing
5 a very nice, new coat. The thief had an idea, and he sat down beside the hotelkeeper. They talked about the weather and about the town. Then the thief opened his mouth wide—a very big yawn. And right after that, he howled like a wolf.

The hotelkeeper asked him, "Why do you howl like a wolf?"
10 "I will tell you," said the thief. "But first, please hold my jacket." The thief took it off.

"I will gladly hold your jacket," said the hotelkeeper. "But why?"

"So I won't tear it to pieces," said the thief. "When I yawn for the third time, I turn into a wolf, and I attack everything." Then the thief yawned a
15 second time, and again howled like a wolf.

The hotelkeeper jumped up from his chair. He started to run away, but the thief got hold of his nice, new coat.

The thief said, "Wait, sir!" and then he started to yawn and howl a third
20 time.

The hotelkeeper was very frightened. He pulled away from the thief and left his coat in the thief's hands. Then he ran inside the hotel
25 and closed the door with a bang.

The thief put on the hotelkeeper's nice, new coat and walked away.

(one of Aesop's Fables from Greece)

C. *Read the fable again and underline the new words. Then choose four new words you want to learn. Look them up and wirte them with their meanings.*

Words	Meanings
_____	_____
_____	_____
_____	_____
_____	_____

D. *Read the fable a third time. Then talk about it with another student. (See the questions on page 6.)*

E. *Write the new words and meanings from Exercise C in your vocabulary notebook.*

Fable 3

A. *Preview the fable.*

B. *Read the fable to the end.*

Sinbad and the Genie

One day Sinbad the Sailor was at the seaside. He sat down by the water. Somebody called to him. He looked around.
5   There were no people nearby, but there was an old bottle. He looked at the bottle. In it, there was a very, very small person. It was a genie.
10   "Help! Help!" cried the genie. "Please let me out."
Sinbad opened the bottle. A big, gray cloud came out. In the cloud, there was a very,
15   very big genie.

(continued)

"Thank you, sailor. I was in that bottle for a long time, and now I'm very hungry. My last meal was 5,000 years ago. I think I'll eat *you*!"

The genie was very big and strong and he had Sinbad in his hand, but Sinbad was clever.

20   He said to the genie, "How can you eat me—a little thing like you?"

"Little?" said the genie, in an angry voice. "I'm not little. I'm very big!"

"How can you be very big?" asked Sinbad. "You were in this little bottle!"

"I was little, and now I'm big," said the genie. "Can't you see how big I am?"

"No, no," said Sinbad. "I see only a little bottle."

25   The genie was angry. His face was all red. He looked terrible. "I'll show you!" he shouted. "Look at me! I'll change in front of your eyes again!"

The big, gray cloud came back around the genie. Then the cloud and the genie got smaller and smaller. Soon the genie was little again, and he climbed into the bottle.

30   Sinbad quickly put the top on the bottle. He threw the bottle into the sea. "Goodbye for another 5,000 years," he said, and he walked away.

(a fable from the Middle East)

C. **Read the fable again and underline the new words. Then choose four new words you want to learn. Look them up and write them with their meanings.**

Words	Meanings
_____	_____
_____	_____
_____	_____
_____	_____

D. **Read the fable a third time. Then talk about it with another student. (See the questions on page 6.)**

E. **Write the new words and meanings from Exercise C in your vocabulary notebook.**

Fable 4

A. *Preview the fable.*

B. *Read the fable to the end.*

The Big Family in the Little House

Once there was a man with a big family. He lived in a very small house on a farm. He wasn't very happy. "We can't live this way!" he said to his wife.

He went to town to talk to his aunt. She was a wise woman, and she always knew what to do. "Please help me," he said. "We have six children now. Eight
5   people in just a few rooms! We can never be happy in such a little house. What can I do?"

His aunt listened. She closed her eyes for a minute. Then she asked, "How many animals do you have on your farm?"

"We have a lot of animals," said the man. "We have a horse, a cow, two pigs,
10   and ten chickens."

"Good," said his aunt. "Take all those animals in your house with you."

"In the house!" said the man. But he went home and did what his aunt told him.

The next week, he went back to see his aunt again.
15   "This is terrible!" he said. "The animals eat our food. They fill all the rooms. They sleep in our beds. They are dirty and noisy. We can't live this way!"

His aunt listened and closed her eyes again. Then she said, "Now go home and take the animals out of your house."

The man went home and took the animals out of the house.
20   The next week, he went back once again to see his aunt. This time he was happy. "Thank you, thank you for your help," he said. "Now we like our house. You are a very wise woman."

(a Jewish fable from Eastern Europe)

C. *Read the fable again and underline the new words. Then choose four new words you want to learn. Look them up and write them with their meanings.*

Words	Meanings
_____	_____
_____	_____
_____	_____
_____	_____

D. *Read the fable a third time. Then talk about it with another student. (See the questions on page 6.)*

E. *Write the new words and meanings from Exercise C in your vocabulary notebook.*

Fable 5

A. *Preview the fable.*

B. *Read the fable to the end.*

The Farm Girl and the Milk

Once there was a girl who lived on a farm. Every day she took care of the cows. She milked them, and then she made butter and cheese. One morning her father said, "You are a good girl. You work very hard. You can have some of the milk this morning. You can take it to town and sell it at the market. Then you can keep the money and buy something nice."

The farm girl started on the road to town with the milk. On the way, she thought, "This is good milk. I can sell it for a good price.
Then I can buy some eggs. I'll bring those eggs home and keep them. Soon I'll have chickens. Chickens grow fast. In a few months, I'll have more eggs and more chickens. Then I can sell the chickens and keep the money. In a few more months, I'll have enough money for a new dress."

The farm girl could see the town now. It was not far away. "I'll buy a beautiful dress," she thought. "It will be blue and gold. It will be the most beautiful dress in town. All the young men will look at me. But I won't talk to any of the young men in town. I'll wait for a rich man or a prince to come by. Yes, a prince. He'll see me and fall in love. I'll marry a prince."

The farm girl was very happy. She closed her eyes, thinking about the prince. She didn't see a large stone in the road. Her foot hit the stone, and down she went. Down went the milk, too — all over the road. And that was the end of the eggs, the chickens, the dress, and the prince.

(one of Aesop's Fables from Greece)

C. Read the fable again and underline the new words. Then choose four new words you want to learn. Look them up and write them with their meanings.

Words   Meanings

_____   _____

_____   _____

_____   _____

_____   _____

D. Read the fable a third time. Then talk about it with another student. (See the questions on page 6.)

E. Write the new words and meanings from Exercise C in your vocabulary notebook.

Fable 6

A. Preview the fable.

B. Read the fable to the end.

The Boy and the Wolf

Once there was a boy who lived in a village. Every day he went out to the fields with his father's sheep. He stayed with the sheep all day. In the evening, he came back to the village.

One day the boy thought, "I don't like this job! I'm alone all day with these
5   sheep. I don't see or talk to people all day."

He sat there for some time. Then he had an idea. He jumped up and began to shout.

"Wolf! Wolf!"

In a few minutes, people came running from the village.
10   "Where is the wolf?" they asked.

"Oh, there's no wolf," said the boy. "I was lonely, and I just wanted to talk to somebody."

"Bad boy!" said the people. They went back to the village.

The next day, the boy went out with his father's sheep. He stayed there with
15   the sheep all morning. But in the afternoon, he wanted to see people again.

"Wolf! Wolf!" he shouted.

Again the people came running from the village. They soon learned that there was no wolf. They were very angry. "Don't do that again!" they said.

"Next time we won't come. We have work to do. We can't come here to talk to
20   you!" And they went back to the village.

(continued)

Later that same afternoon, the boy heard a noise. It came from the forest nearby. Then he saw something behind the trees. It was a big gray wolf.

"Help! Help!" shouted the boy. "There's a wolf!"

The people in the village heard the boy, but this time they didn't come.

25   The boy climbed up a tree, and he couldn't save the sheep from the hungry wolf.

(one of Aesop's Fables from Greece)

C. **Read the fable again and underline the new words. Then choose four new words you want to learn. Look them up and write them with their meanings.**

Words	Meanings
_____	_____
_____	_____
_____	_____
_____	_____

D. **Read the fable a third time. Then talk about it with another student. (See the questions on page 6.)**

E. **Write the new words and meanings from Exercise C in your vocabulary notebook.**

Fable 7

A. *Preview the fable.*

B. *Read the fable to the end.*

The Farmer, the Boy, and the Horse

Once there was a farmer who wanted to sell his horse in town. One morning he started down the road with the horse and his young son. He and his son walked beside the horse. They passed some boys.

"Why is that man walking?" said one of the boys. "He has a horse! Why
5 isn't he riding the horse?"

The farmer heard the boy. "He's right," the farmer said. "I'll get on the horse." He got on the horse, and his son walked beside him. They passed some women.

"Look at that man!" said one of the women. "He's on the horse, and his
10 poor boy is walking."

"She's right," said the farmer. He got down from the horse, and he put his son on it. They walked some more. They passed an old man.

"Look at that boy!" said the old man. "Young people have no love for their parents these days! There he sits on the horse, and his poor father has to walk."
15 "He's right," said the farmer. He got on the horse behind his son. Then they passed some girls.

"Two people on a horse!" said the girls. "The poor animal!"

"They're right," said the farmer. He and his son got off the horse. He put the horse on his back and started down the road.

20 They came to a bridge over a river. Some people were fishing from the bridge. "Look at that!" they
said. "A man carrying a horse!"
They laughed and laughed.

The horse was not happy.
25 He began to move and kick.
Soon the horse, the farmer,
and his son all fell off the
bridge and into the river. The
horse ran home. The farmer
30 and his son climbed out of the
river.

"Next time," said the
farmer. "I won't listen to other
people. I'll do it my way."

(one of Aesop's Fables from Greece)

C. Read the fable again and underline the new words. Then choose four new words you want to learn. Look them up and write them with their meanings.

Words	Meanings
_____	_____
_____	_____
_____	_____

D. Read the fable a third time. Then talk about it with another student. (See the questions on page 6.)

E. Write the new words and meanings from Exercise C in your vocabulary notebook.

Fable 8

A. Preview the fable.

B. Read the fable to the end.

The Wolf and the Dog

One evening a very hungry wolf came to a farm. He saw some chickens in the farmyard. He wanted to eat the chickens, but there was a dog in the yard, too. The dog was big and strong. The wolf didn't want to have a fight with the dog. So he waited just outside the yard.

5 After a while, a man came out of the farmhouse. He put some food out for the dog and then went back into the house.

"Good evening," the wolf called to the dog.

"Good evening," said the dog with his mouth full.

The wolf said, "Do you get that much food every day?"

"Two times a day," said the dog. "I get breakfast in the morning and dinner
10 in the evening." He ate some more. Then he looked at the wolf and asked "Are you hungry?"

"Very hungry," said the wolf.

"Why don't you come live here with me?" said the dog. This is a good life. I watch the chickens for the farmer, and he gives me food."

15 The wolf sat down near the dog. He thought, "Why not? If I stay here, I don't have to go hunting every night. He's right. It's an easy life."

But then he looked at the dog.

What's that under your ears?" he asked.

"What?" said the dog.

20   "Look at your neck! It's all red!" said the wolf.

       "Oh, that's nothing," said the dog.

       "But doesn't it hurt? What's it from?"

       "It's just the chain," said the dog. "During the day, the farmer puts a chain on my neck."

25   "A chain!" said the wolf. "You have to wear a chain all day!"

       "That's right," said the dog. "But I don't care. I sleep all day, and in the evening he takes it off."

       "Then no, thank you, my friend," said the wolf. "I don't want a chain around my neck. Not even for a minute! Goodbye!"

30   And the wolf ran away, still hungry.

(one of Aesop's Fables from Greece)

C. **Read the fable again and underline the new words. Then choose four new words you want to learn. Look them up and write them with their meanings.**

Words	Meanings
_____	_____
_____	_____
_____	_____
_____	_____

D. **Read the fable a third time. Then talk about it with another student. (See the questions on page 6.)**

E. **Write the new words and meanings from Exercise C in your vocabulary notebook.**

Fable 9

A. **Preview the fable.**

B. **Read the fable to the end.**

The Old Woman and the Doctor

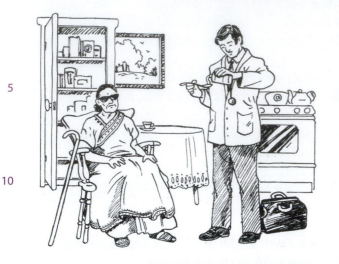

An old woman suddenly could not see anymore. She went to a doctor.

"Please help me," she said. "I'm blind. I want to see."

The doctor gave her medicine, and she paid him some money. But the medicine didn't help her. She still couldn't see.

She went to another doctor. "Please, please help me," she said. "I don't want to be blind."

This doctor gave her different medicine. The old woman paid him even more money. She took the medicine for a long time, but she still couldn't see.

Then a new doctor came to town. The old woman went to see him.

"Please, Doctor, please make my eyes better. I'm very unhappy. I want to see."

The doctor said, "I can make your eyes better, but you have to pay me a lot of money."

"First make my eyes better," said the old woman, "and then I will pay you."

Every day the doctor went to the woman's house. He took care of her and gave her medicine. But this doctor was also a thief. Every day he took something away from the woman's house. First, he took some boxes of food. Then he took some paintings from the walls. Then he even took the tables and chairs.

But the medicine he gave her was good medicine. After some time, the old woman could see again. She was not blind any more.

"Now," said the doctor. "Give me the money."

"No," said the woman. "I won't give you any money."

So the doctor went to a judge and said, "She was blind, and now she is better, but she won't pay me for my medicine."

The judge turned to the old woman and said, "Why is this?"

The old woman said, "I told the doctor I would pay him when I could see well, but I can't see well. Before I was blind, I could see boxes of food, paintings, tables, and chairs in my house. Now I see nothing but the walls. So my eyes are not really better."

The judge smiled and understood. "Doctor," he said, "She is right. Her eyes are not better if she can't see the boxes and tables and chairs. When she can see all those things in her house again, she will pay you."

That night the doctor went to the woman's house and put all the things back.

(a fable from India)

C. *Read the fable again and underline the new words. Then choose four new words you want to learn. Look them up and write them with their meanings.*

<table>
<tr><td align="center">**Words**</td><td align="center">**Meanings**</td></tr>
<tr><td>_____</td><td>_____</td></tr>
<tr><td>_____</td><td>_____</td></tr>
<tr><td>_____</td><td>_____</td></tr>
<tr><td>_____</td><td>_____</td></tr>
</table>

D. *Read the fable a third time. Then talk about it with another student. (See the questions on page 6.)*

E. *Write the new words and meanings from Exercise C in your vocabulary notebook.*

Fable 10

A. *Preview the fable.*

B. *Read the fable to the end.*

Monkey Looks for Trouble

One day Monkey was in a treetop near a road. He saw a woman walking along the road to town. She was carrying some cakes in a pot. She didn't see a stone in the road, so she fell down. The pot broke, and all the cakes fell onto the road.

5 "Oh, no!" she cried. She looked at the cakes. "What a lot of trouble! Trouble, trouble, nothing but trouble!" She left the cakes on the road and went back home.

10 Monkey came down from the tree. He looked at the cakes on the road.
He smelled them and said to himself, "These are trouble? They

15 look good to eat. They smell very good." He put one in his mouth, and it was very good. Soon he ate all of the cakes.

(continued)

"That trouble was so good," said Monkey. "I must find more trouble."

20 He ran to the market in town. He stopped at a little shop, "Please," he said to the man, "can I have some trouble?"

The man looked at him. "You're looking for trouble?" he asked. Monkey said, "Yes, yes. I want trouble. All the trouble you have, please."

The man laughed and went to the back of the store. In a few minutes, he 25 came out with a large bag.

"Here you are," he said to Monkey. Monkey paid him and then started down the road. It was not easy for Monkey to carry the bag. It was large and heavy. It also jumped around a lot. But Monkey was happy to have his trouble.

He went down the road to a quiet place. He was ready to eat his trouble. 30 He opened the bag, and out came three angry dogs. Monkey ran away and climbed up a tree. The dogs ran after him, making a lot of noise. They stayed under the tree for a long time.

Monkey began to get hungry. He saw some fruit in the tree. He took a nice red fruit and put it into his mouth. "O-o-w!" he cried. "O-o-w!" The tree was a 35 pepper tree, and the fruit was a very hot pepper. Monkey's mouth burned, and he wanted some water. But the dogs were still under the tree. He waited and waited until at last, the dogs went away.

Then Monkey climbed down from the tree and drank some water. He never looked for trouble again.

(a fable from Trinidad)

C. *Read the fable again and underline the new words. Then choose four new words you want to learn. Look them up and write them with their meanings.*

Words	Meanings
_____	_____
_____	_____
_____	_____
_____	_____

D. *Read the fable a third time. Then talk about it with another student. (See the questions on page 6.)*

E. *Write the new words and meanings from Exercise C in your vocabulary notebook.*

Fable 11

A. **Preview the fable.**

B. **Read the fable to the end.**

The Marriage of the Mouse Princess

Once there was a mouse princess. She was very beautiful, and she was in love with a young mouse. But her parents, the mouse king and mouse queen, said she couldn't marry the young mouse.

"Our daughter is a princess. She must marry someone special," they said. "She must marry the strongest person in the world."

They went to a wise mouse. "Who's the strongest person in the world?" they asked.

The wise mouse looked up at the sky. "The sun makes the rice grow. The sun is the strongest person in the world."

So the mouse king and queen went to the home of the sun, "O Sun! You are the strongest person in the world. Will you marry our daughter?"

"Your daughter is very beautiful," said the sun. "But I'm not the person you are looking for. The cloud is stronger than me. He can take away my light."

So the mouse king and queen went to home of the cloud. "O Cloud!" they said. "You are the strongest person in the world. Will you marry our daughter?"

The cloud answered, "No, no. You are wrong. I am not the strongest person in the world. The wind is stronger. I must go where he tells me."

So the mouse king and queen went to the home of the wind. "O Wind!" they said. "Please, we are looking for the strongest person in the world to marry our daughter. Are you that person?"

The wind laughed and said, "I am very strong, but not the strongest. Do you see that high wall over there? He is stronger because I cannot make him move."

The mouse king and queen went to the wall. It was quite near to their home. The wall was not happy to see them. "What do you want?" he said.

"The wind says you are the strongest person in the world," they said. "Will you marry our daughter?"

"I'm not the strongest person in the world, and I will not marry your daughter!" said the wall. "Look at me, down near the ground. Do you see all those holes? The mouse made those holes. Some day soon, I'll fall down because of those holes. You should ask the mouse to marry your daughter."

The mouse king and queen went to the home of the mouse. It was the same young mouse their daughter loved. He was happy to marry their daughter, and she was very happy to marry him.

(a fable from Japan)

C. *Read the fable again and underline the new words. Then choose four new words you want to learn. Look them up and write them with their meanings.*

Words	Meanings
_____	_____
_____	_____
_____	_____
_____	_____

D. *Read the fable a third time. Then talk about it with another student. (See the questions on page 6.)*

E. *Write the new words and meanings from Exercise C in your vocabulary notebook.*

Fable 12

A. *Preview the fable.*

B. *Read the fable to the end.*

Tiger and the Big Wind

One year it didn't rain. There wasn't much food or water, and all the animals were very hungry and thirsty.

In the middle of the forest, where the animals lived, there was a field. In this field, there was a large pear tree. It was full of pears—big, yellow pears that were ready to eat. But none of the animals could eat the pears because
5   there was a tiger under the pear tree. He didn't want to eat the pears because, of course, tigers don't eat fruit! But he also didn't want the other animals to eat the pears. When the monkeys tried to come near the tree, the tiger made a terrible sound. "Stay away or I'll eat you up!" he shouted.

The animals didn't know what to do. Then along came Rabbit. "Oh,
10 Rabbit, you're so clever. What are we to do? We're so hungry and thirsty, but Tiger won't let us eat the pears," said the animals.

Rabbit thought for a while and then he had an idea. "Come close, my friends. Listen to me and I'll tell you what to do."

Very early the next morning, all the animals were in the forest near the
15 field. The birds and the monkeys sat in the trees. The other animals hid behind the trees. The tiger was still sleeping.

Soon Rabbit came along, carrying a large, thick rope. He ran across the field and made a lot of noise. Tiger opened one eye and said angrily, "Why are you making so much noise? Can't you see I'm sleeping?"

20 "Tiger!" shouted Rabbit. "You must run! A big wind is coming. It will blow everything and everyone off the earth."

At that moment, all the animals in the forest began to make noise. The birds and the monkeys jumped around the tops of the trees. The elephants and other big animals made the trees shake and move. Soon the whole forest was

25 shaking and moving. It sounded like the end of the world.

Tiger was afraid. "What should I do?" he cried.

"You must run," said Rabbit. "I can't help you now. I have to go tie down the other animals with this rope. If I don't, the wind will blow them away."

"You must tie me down," said Tiger.

30 But Rabbit said, "No, I must help the other animals. You are big and strong. You can run far and get away."

"No!" shouted Tiger. "You must tie ME down now."

"Okay, okay," said Rabbit. "I will tie you down now."

And so he tied Tiger to a tree near the field.

35 "More rope, more rope!" said Tiger. "I don't want to blow away!"

Rabbit got more rope and tied it around and around Tiger.

40 When he finished, he called to his friends in the forest.

"Come on out!" he called. "Look at this. Look at Tiger. Now he can't keep us away from the pears."

45 Then all the animals came out of the forest. They sat happily together under the pear tree and ate all the

50 pears.

(a fable from Africa)

C. **Read the fable again and underline the new words. Then choose four new words you want to learn. Look them up and write them with their meanings.**

Words	Meanings
_____	_____
_____	_____
_____	_____
_____	_____

D. *Read the fable a third time. Then talk about it with another student. (See the questions on page 6.)*

E. *Write the new words and meanings from Exercise C in your vocabulary notebook.*

Fable 13

A. *Preview the fable.*

B. *Read the fable to the end.*

The Spider and the Turtle

One evening Spider was about to have dinner. He had some very nice, hot yams (sweet potatoes) to eat. He heard a knock on the door. It was Turtle, who was returning from a long trip. He was very tired and very hungry.

"Could I please have some of your yams?" he asked Spider. "They smell so good."

Spider did not want to give Turtle any yams. He wanted to eat them all himself. But he didn't want people to say bad things about him. So he said, "Come in, my friend. Come sit down and have some yams."

But when Turtle put out a hand to take some food, Spider said, "Wait! Look at your hands. They're very dirty! In this country, people wash their hands before they eat. Please go wash yours."

It was true. Turtle's hands were dirty from his long trip. He went down to the river to wash them. While he was out, Spider began eating. When Turtle came back, half the yams were gone. He sat down. He was again about to take some yams, when Spider said, "Stop! Your hands are dirty again."

Turtle looked at his hands. He used them for walking, of course. And they had gotten dirty on the way back from the river. He went out to the river again. This time he walked back on the grass. But when he sat down at Spider's table again, there were no more yams. Spider had eaten them all.

Turtle looked at Spider for a moment. Then he said, "Thank you for inviting me to dinner. You must come to my house for dinner some day." Then he left the house and slowly went on his way.

A few days later, Spider was hungry. He had no more yams. He
35 remembered Turtle's words. "Why not?" he thought. "I'll have a free meal." So the next day, Spider went to visit Turtle. He found him near his home in the river.

"Well, hello," said Turtle. "Would you like to have dinner with me?"

"Oh, yes, yes," said Spider. He was very hungry.

40 "Just a moment then," said Turtle. He dived down into the river. In a few minutes, he returned. "Please come," he said to Spider. "Dinner is ready." Turtle went back down to his home and began to eat.

Spider jumped into the river, but he didn't go down into the water. He stayed on top. He was too light. He tried and tried to swim down, but he
45 always popped back up again. Then he had an idea. He put some rocks in the pockets of his jacket. This time he swam down and stayed down.

Spider sat at the table with Turtle. There were all kinds of good things to eat. Just as Spider was about to take some food, Turtle said to him, "In my country, people don't eat with their jackets on. Could you please take off your
50 jacket?" Turtle's jacket was on the back of his chair.

"Of course," said Spider. But the moment he took off his jacket, he popped up out of the water. He put his head underwater and looked down. There was Turtle slowly eating all the food on the table.

(a fable from Africa)

C. **Read the fable again and underline the new words. Then choose four new words you want to learn. Look them up and write them with their meanings.**

Words	Meanings
_____	_____
_____	_____
_____	_____
_____	_____

D. **Read the fable a third time. Then talk about it with another student. (See the questions on page 6.)**

E. **Write the new words and meanings from Exercise C in your vocabulary notebook.**

Fable 14

A. Preview the fable.

B. Read the fable to the end.

The Fisherman and His Wife

Once there was a fisherman. He and his wife lived in a little house by the sea. They were very poor. One day he went out fishing. He waited and waited for fish all day. Then, finally, he caught a big, fat fish. Before he could kill it, the fish spoke to him.

5   "Please put me back into the sea," it said. "I am not like other fish. I can do magic. Tell me what you want, and I can give it to you."

The fisherman couldn't think of anything. He put the fish back into the sea and went home. He told his wife about the fish. "What!" she said. "You didn't ask for anything! Our house is old. Go ask for a new house."

10   The fisherman went back to the sea. He called to the fish, "O Fish! Please listen to me."

The fish came near. "What do you want?" he said.

"My wife wants a new house," said the fisherman.

"Go home," said the fish. "Your wife has a new house."

15   The fisherman went home. His wife was in a nice, new house with flowers on all the windows. She was very happy.

But the next morning, she said to her husband, "This house is very small. I want a bigger house. Go ask for a bigger house."

The fisherman went to the sea again. "O Fish," he called. "Please listen to

20 me."

The fish came near. "What do you want?" he asked.

"I like our little house," he said. "But my wife wants a bigger house."

25   "Go home," said the fish. "Your wife has a big house."

The fisherman went home. His wife was in a very big house. There were many

30 beautiful things in it and a large garden around it. The fisherman asked his wife, "Are you happy now?" "Oh, yes," she said.

But the next morning she

35 said, "This house is nice, but I want more. I want to be queen. Then I will be happy."

"He gave us a new house and a big house," said the fisherman. "He won't listen to me now."

40   "Yes, he will!" said his wife. "Tell him I must be queen!"

So the fisherman went back to the sea again. "O Fish!" he called. "Please listen to me."

The fish came near. "What do you want?" he said.

"My wife says she wants to be queen," said the fisherman.

45   "Go home," said the fish. "Your wife is now queen."

The fisherman went home. His wife was queen. She had on a beautiful dress of gold. She had a gold crown on her head.

"Now you can be happy," said the fisherman.

"Maybe," said his wife.

50   The next morning, it was raining. The fisherman's wife said to her husband, "I don't like this rain. Go tell the fish I want to stop the rain. Tell him I want the sun."

"I can't go back again," said the fisherman. "Don't you have enough?" But she only laughed.

55   So he went back to the sea another time. "O Fish!" he called. "Please listen to me."

The fish came near. "What do you want?" he said.

"Please help me!" said the fisherman. "My wife is still not happy. She wants to stop the rain. She wants the sun."

60   "Go home," said the fish. "Your wife asks for too much! Now she has nothing!"

The fisherman went home. His wife was in their little, old house again. And once again, they were very poor.

(a fable from Germany by the Brothers Grimm)

C.   ***Read the fable again and underline the new words. Then choose four new words you want to learn. Look them up and write them with their meanings.***

Words	Meanings
_____	_____
_____	_____
_____	_____
_____	_____

D.   ***Read the fable a third time. Then talk about it with another student. (See the questions on page 6.)***

E.   ***Write the new words and meanings from Exercise C in your vocabulary notebook.***

Stories

Some of these stories are nonfiction. They are true stories about real people and events. Other stories are fiction. They are not about real people or events.

Follow these steps when you are reading the stories:

1. **Preview the story.**
   - Read the title and look at the picture (if there is one).
   - Look quickly through the story.
   - What do you think the story is about?

2. **Read the story to the end.**
   - Don't stop to look up new words in the dictionary.

3. **Read the story again. Underline the new words.**
   - Write the new words below the story.
   - Look them up in the dictionary. Write the meanings beside the words.

4. **Read the story a third time. Then talk about these questions with another student.**
   - What and who is the story about? Where does it take place?
   - What did you learn from this story?
   - Do you like the story? Why or why not?
   - Is it like any other story you have read? If so, explain.

5. **Write the new words and their meanings in your vocabulary notebook. (See Part 2, Unit 1, page 71.)**

Story 1

The Man with the Gloves

Michael Greenberg lived in New York City. Every day he walked to work. He walked fast, like the other people in New York. He looked down at the ground. He didn't look at other people in the street.

One winter morning, Michael was late for work. He walked very fast
5   around a corner. He ran into an old man, and the man fell down. Michael stopped to help him. The old man didn't have warm clothes. Michael saw his hands. They were blue with cold!

Michael took off his gloves and gave them to the old man. The old man looked at the gloves, and he looked at Michael. Then he put the gloves on his hands. Michael said goodbye. The old man just looked at the gloves and smiled.

That evening, Michael had no gloves. His hands got very cold. He looked around the streets, and he saw other people with no gloves. They were poor people, and they had no homes. They stayed on the streets all day, and some of them slept on the streets at night. Michael wanted to help these people. What could he do? He went to a store and bought some gloves.

The next morning, he saw a woman with no gloves. He opened his bag and took out some gloves. The woman said no, she didn't have money for gloves. But Michael put the gloves on her hands. She had two children with her. He gave them gloves, too. The gloves were very big, but the children were happy with them. Michael bought more gloves that evening. He bought big gloves for men and women and little gloves for children. The next day, he gave them all away. After that, he always had gloves in his bag in the winter. The homeless people soon knew Michael well. They called him "Gloves" Greenberg. "Here comes Gloves," they said.

And so, for more than 25 years, Michael gave gloves to the poor people in New York. A pair of gloves is a small thing. But it can make a big difference to people in New York during the winter.

(a true story)

Words	Meanings
_____	_____
_____	_____
_____	_____
_____	_____

Story 2

Christmas Gifts

Many years ago, Jim and Della lived in New York City. They were poor, but they were young, and they were in love. It was the day before Christmas. Every year, they had a nice dinner on Christmas. Then they opened their presents. They couldn't buy expensive things, but they always gave each other something.

But this year, Jim and Della still had no presents. Jim didn't have a job, so they didn't have much money. "We don't need presents," they said. "We're happy without them." But it wasn't true. Jim wanted to buy something for Della, and she wanted to buy something for him.

10   In the morning, Jim went to look for a job. Della went into town. She had only $1.87 with her. What could she buy for $1.87? She looked at the store windows. There were many beautiful things, but they were all expensive. In one window, there were many watches. There was also a very nice gold watch chain. "Just right for Jim's watch," thought Della. But it cost $21.

15   Jim and Della were poor, but they did have two beautiful things. Jim had a gold watch from his father. Della had very long, beautiful red hair. Now in the store window, she could see her face and hair, and she had an idea. She went to a hairdresser.

"How much will you give me for my hair?" she asked.

20   The hairdresser looked at Della's hair and said, "twenty dollars."

"Okay, it's yours," said Della.

When she came back home, Jim was there, too.

"Look at me!" Della said. "Do you like my new haircut?"

"Oh, no!" cried Jim.

25   "You don't like it?" said Della.

"Why did you do that?" asked Jim.

"I wanted to buy something for you," said Della. "Here it is!"

John opened the present. "Oh, Della," he said. "This is terrible."

"You don't like it?"

30   "No, no. Thank you. It's a wonderful chain," said Jim. "But I don't have a watch now. I sold it to my friend George. I wanted to get these."

Della opened a small box. In it there were two combs for her hair. They were very beautiful, but now her hair was too short. She couldn't use combs!

35   "I can use them next year," she said. "Thank you, my love."

"George said I can buy my watch when I have the money," Jim said. "I know I'll get a job soon, and then I'll get my watch back."

40   Jim smiled. "You know, Della," he said, "you're beautiful with short hair!"

(adapted from a story by O. Henry)

Words	Meanings
_____	_____
_____	_____
_____	_____
_____	_____

The Man Who Could Paint Like Picasso

John Myatt was a painter in England. He was married, and he had two little children. Then one day, his wife fell in love with another man. She left him and the children.

Now John was alone with the children. His didn't get much money from his job at an art school. He couldn't take another job because of the children. He needed a job that he could do at home.

Art was something he could do at home. But he was not a famous painter. His paintings did not sell for a lot of money. Then he remembered the Picasso.

Some years before, a rich friend wanted to buy a painting by Picasso. It cost many thousands of dollars. John said, "Don't buy it. I'll make you a Picasso." So he did. He painted a picture that looked just like a real Picasso. His friend paid John a few hundred dollars and put it in his living room.

This was something John could do. He could paint just like any famous painter—like Picasso, Van Gogh, Matisse. So he decided to make money this way, with copies of famous pictures. He signed his name on all of the paintings. He didn't want people to think they were really by famous artists.

Then a man named Drewe bought some of John's paintings. A short time later, he bought some more, and then more. He paid John well for them. John understood that Drewe was not putting all the pictures in his living room. But he didn't tell John what he was doing, and John didn't ask.

After six years, John decided to stop selling pictures to Drewe. He didn't like the man, and he had enough money. But it was too late. The police knew about Drewe. They soon came to John's house. Then he learned from the police what Drewe did with his paintings. He took John's name off them, and he sold them as paintings by famous artists. Everyone thought they were real. They paid a lot of money for them.

But they were John's paintings, so John had to go to jail for four months. When he came out, he was famous, too. The newspapers wrote about him. People wanted to know how he did his paintings.

After that, he went to work for the police and helped them find copies of famous art. He also had a big show in London of his paintings. They were copies of famous pictures. Now, of course, they had his name on them. But he sold them all for a lot of money.

(a true story)

Words	Meanings
_____	_____
_____	_____
_____	_____
_____	_____

The Telephone Call

Camille was three years old. She lived in a small town in France. Her father worked in the city. Her mother worked in the house.

One Saturday Camille's mother fell onto the floor. She lay on the floor without moving. Her eyes were closed. She didn't open her eyes when Camille
5 called her. But Camille's father was home. He called the doctor. The doctor came quickly and gave Camille's mother some medicine. In a few days, she was well again.

Then one day, she fell down again. This time, Camille's father was not home. There was only Camille. She called her mother, but her mother didn't
10 answer. Camille was afraid and started to cry. Then she remembered what her father did. She did the same thing. She went to the telephone, and she pushed some numbers.

A man answered her call. He was an engineer named Claude Armand. His office was in the city. He didn't know Camille, and at first, he didn't
15 understand her. But he had children, and he understood there was a problem.

Camille cried, "Mommy, Mommy!"

"Where's your mother?" asked the engineer.

"She's lying down," said Camille. "She can't get up." And she started to cry.

"Don't cry, don't cry," said the engineer. "We'll help your mother. First you
20 need to tell me some things. Where do you live?"

"Near my grandma," said Camille. But she didn't know her street or her town. She was only three years old!

"Tell me more," said the engineer. "Talk to me some more." At the same time, he wrote a message to a friend in his office, "This little girl needs help!"
25 the message said. "Call the telephone company and find out her address!"

Now the engineer had to keep Camille on the phone. "Tell me about your daddy," he asked. "Where is he?"

"At work," said Camille.

Then he asked her lots more questions. Camille was happy to talk to
30 someone. They talked about her house and her family. She told him about her grandparents, her friends, and her little cat. They talked for 25 minutes!

And while they talked, the engineer's friend called the telephone company. She told them about Camille's mother. The telephone company told the police. The police told the government in Paris. The government said okay. And the
35 telephone company told the police Camille's address.

All this time, Camille talked with the engineer. Then the police came to Camille's house with a doctor. They called to her and rang the doorbell. Camille said goodbye to Claude Armand and went to open the door. Now she was not alone anymore. Now her mother was okay.

(a true story)

Words	Meanings
_____	_____
_____	_____
_____	_____
_____	_____

Story 5

A Day Trip to Mexico

Seattle is a city by the sea. There are lots of boats in Seattle. Some of the boats are fishing boats. Some boats go to faraway places. Some boats go to the San Juan Islands nearby.

5   Anthony Brewer lived in Seattle. He was 16 years old, and he wanted to go away. It was the end of the school year, and it was hot. Anthony's friends were on the San Juan Islands. He wanted to go there, too.

One morning, Anthony had an idea. He didn't tell his
10   parents about his idea. They were at work. He went down to the boats. He couldn't buy a ticket for the San Juan Islands. He didn't have very much money. He walked by the boats. Which one went to the San Juan Islands? He didn't want to ask because he didn't want people to see him.

15   Then he saw a sign on a boat. It said, "San Juan." Anthony looked around. He didn't see any people, so he got on the boat. There were some large boxes on the boat. He got into a box and closed it. After a few minutes, he heard some men on the boat. Soon the boat started to move. Through some holes in the boxes, Anthony could look out. He saw the buildings of Seattle, and then
20   he saw only the sea.

Anthony was happy to be on the boat. It moved up and down a little. He was comfortable in the box, and it was a warm day. Soon he was asleep.

When he woke up, he looked at his watch. It was two hours later. He looked around and saw only the sea. Why were they still at sea? The San Juan Islands
25   were only an hour from Seattle. He listened to the people on the boat, but he could not understand them. They weren't speaking English. Maybe this wasn't the boat for the San Juan Islands! What boat was it? Where was it going?

Anthony didn't know what to do. He sat in the box all day. Night came, and it was very cold in the box. He had no warm clothing, no food, and
30   nothing to drink. Now he wanted to go home!

The next morning, some men opened the box. They saw Anthony, and they pulled him out. Anthony was afraid. But the men smiled.

"Where is this boat going?" he asked.

(continued)

"To Mexico," they answered.

35 "Mexico!" he cried. "Can't you stop somewhere? I have to go home!"

"No," they said. "We can't stop. But we can call your parents."

And so they did. They also gave him food and a place to sleep. Ten days later, Anthony was in Mexico. He went to the Mexican police for help. They put him on a plane to Seattle. His parents came to get him at the airport. They

40 had to pay for the airplane ticket. But they weren't angry with him. They were happy to see him again.

(fiction)

Words	Meanings
_____	_____
_____	_____
_____	_____
_____	_____

Story 6

Read a Book—or Go to Jail!

Stan Rosen lived in New Bedford, Massachusetts. He stole cars and bicycles from people, and he sold them again. That was how he made a living. One day, the police caught him and sent him to jail.

The next year, Stan was out of jail. He told some people his name was Jim

5 Rosen. He got money from them to start a business. Then he ran away with the money. After some months, the police caught him again and sent him to jail.

The year after that, Stan was home again. He didn't have a job, and he didn't have any money. One night, he stole some money from a store. Again, the police caught him. But this time, they sent him to Judge Kane.

10 Judge Kane asked Stan, "Do you want to go to jail again? Or do you want to read books?"

Stan didn't understand.

"This time," said the judge, "you can decide. There is a new course at New Bedford High School. It's for people like you. You're 27 years old. You never

15 finished school. You don't have a job. You steal things. But you never hurt anyone. So you can take the course and read books with Professor Waxler. Or you can go to jail."

Stan didn't read much. He didn't like reading! But he didn't want to go to jail again. So he decided to read books in Professor Waxler's class. "You must

20 go to every class," said the judge. "And you must read all the books."

Stan went to the first class. There were ten men in the class. All the men were sent by Judge Kane. In the first class, they read a short story.

Professor Waxler asked, "What do you think about it?"

The men said nothing. They didn't know what to say. Stan wanted to
answer the questions, but he was afraid to talk. He didn't want the other men
to hear him.

"Did you like the story?" Professor Waxler asked him.

"No," said Stan.

"Why not?" asked Professor Waxler.

"Because the end was happy, but life isn't happy," said Stan.

"That's not true," said another man. "Life is happy for some people,
sometimes."

Then other men started talking about the story and about life. They talked
for two hours. Professor Waxler told them to read a book for the next class. It
was a book about a young man with many problems.

At the next class, Professor Waxler asked again, "What do you think?"

This time the men were not afraid to answer. They had many things to
say about the book, and they talked a lot about their lives. Many of them had
difficult lives with lots of problems.

For 12 weeks, Stan read books and talked about them. Then he had to
decide again: go to class or go to jail. This time he decided quickly. He wanted
to take another class.

After that, Stan took evening classes at the high school. Judge Kane helped
him find a job for the daytime. The next year, he started evening classes at
the university. Now Stan is a good student—and he has no problems with the
police. Thanks to Judge Kane and Professor Waxler—and some books.

(a true story)

Words	**Meanings**
_____	_____
_____	_____
_____	_____
_____	_____

Story 7

A Man and Many Wolves

Farley Mowat was a scientist. He worked for the Canadian government.
The government wanted to know more about wolves. Do wolves kill lots of
caribou (big animals)? Do they kill people? The government told Farley to
learn about wolves.

(continued)

5   They gave him lots of food and clothes and guns. Then they put him on
a plane and took him to a place in the far north. In this place, there were no
houses or people. But there were lots of animals—and lots of wolves.

  People told terrible stories about wolves. They said wolves liked to kill and
eat people. Farley remembered these stories, and he was afraid. He had his gun
10   with him all the time.

  Then one day, he saw a group of wolves. There was a mother wolf with
four baby wolves. A father wolf and another young wolf lived with them.

  Farley watched these wolves every day. The mother was a very good
mother. She gave milk to her babies. She gave them lessons about life. They
15   learned how to get food. The father wolf got food for the mother. The young
wolf played with the children. They were a nice, happy family—a wolf family!

  In a short time, Farley and the wolf family were friends. He did not need
his gun anymore. Farley watched the wolf family for five months. He learned
many new things about wolves. He learned that many stories about wolves
20   weren't true. Wolves don't eat people, and they don't eat many large animals.
The large animals they eat are often old or sick.

  What do they eat most of the time? Lots of small animals. For example,
Farley saw the wolves catch lots of mice. But can a large animal live on mice?
Farley wanted to know. There was only one way to learn. He was a large animal,
25   too—a large man. He must try to live on mice! So he did. For two weeks, he ate
mice—and no other food. After that he didn't want to eat any more mice! But
he wasn't thin, and he wasn't sick. Yes, a man can live on mice, so a wolf can,
too. Now he could answer the government's questions about wolves.

  In that faraway place, Farley didn't see many people. But he learned some
30   bad things about some hunters. These hunters told terrible stories about
wolves. In the stories, the wolves killed hundreds of caribou. But this wasn't
true. Farley learned that the hunters killed the caribou. They also killed many
wolves.

  Farley Mowat never saw the wolf family again. But he wrote a book about
35   them. The book is called *Never Cry Wolf*. He wanted people to understand
wolves and to stop killing them.

(a true story)

Words	Meanings
_____	_____
_____	_____
_____	_____
_____	_____

Ben and Jerry's

Ben Cohen and Jerry Greenfield both came from Merrick, New York. They were good friends. After college they wanted to start a business together. What kind of business? A food business, of course. Ben and Jerry were different in many ways, but in one way they were the same. They both liked food!

5 One food they liked very much was ice cream. They wanted to open an ice-cream shop. Where was a good place for an ice-cream shop? They looked at many cities and towns. Then they went to Burlington, Vermont. They liked the city a lot. It had lots of young people, and it didn't have any good ice-cream shops. There was only one problem with Burlington. For five months of the

10 year, it was very cold there. Did people buy ice cream on cold days?

On May 5, 1978, Ben and Jerry opened their ice-cream shop. It was a small shop, and it wasn't very beautiful. But the ice cream was very good. Lots of people came to eat ice cream on opening day. They came back again and again. There were

15 always lots of people in the shop. Ben and Jerry worked very hard. One night after work, Ben was so tired that he went to sleep on the ground in front of the shop!

20 After a few months, Ben and Jerry went to the bank. They had bad news. There were only a few dollars in their bank account.

"Why is that?" they asked. "After all these months of hard work!"

Then they started to learn about business. They learned about expenses, marketing, and sales. They started to have big ice-cream parties. They gave free

25 ice cream on some days. People in other cities learned about Ben and Jerry's, and they came a long way to eat the ice cream.

Ben and Jerry made more ice cream, and they started selling it to stores and restaurants. First, they went to stores and restaurants in Vermont. Then they started selling their ice cream to stores across the United States. By 1988

30 they were selling ice cream all over the United States. A few years later, people could also buy their ice cream in Canada, Israel, and many European countries.

Why do people buy Ben and Jerry's ice cream? First of all, it's very good ice cream. It's made with Vermont milk, and it doesn't have any chemicals in it.

People also buy Ben and Jerry's ice cream because they like the company.

35 From the beginning, Ben and Jerry wanted their company to be different. They didn't just want to make a lot of money. They also wanted to try to help people. Ben and Jerry's is now a very big company, but it does help people. It supports farmers in Vermont. It buys lots of milk from them, and that gives the farmers more work. The company also gives lots of jobs to young people and gives

40 7.5% of its profit to help children and sick people around the world.

(a true story)

Words	Meanings
_____	_____
_____	_____
_____	_____
_____	_____

Story 9

The Last Leaf

Sue and Joanna met at a restaurant in New York. Sue was a waitress and Joanna worked in the kitchen. They were both new in New York, and they both wanted to be artists.

Soon they were good friends. They found a small apartment and lived
5 together. They looked for work as artists. But that kind of work was hard to find. Mostly, they worked in the restaurant. And they talked about going to Rome some day. That was their big dream.

The spring went by, and the summer. Then one cold fall day, Joanna didn't feel well. She went to work at the restaurant, but she had to go home early.
10 The next day, she had a terrible cough and a high temperature. She stayed home from work.

That evening Sue said, "We should call a doctor."

"Do you know a doctor?" asked Joanna.

"No," said Sue. "But we can find one."

15 "No, no," said Joanna. "I'll get better. It's just the flu."

But she didn't get better. She got worse and worse. A few days later she was coughing all the time. She had a very high temperature. Sue was afraid.

She called a doctor. When the doctor came, she took a quick look at Joanna. "To the hospital," she said. "Right away."

20 At the hospital, the doctors asked lots of questions and did tests. They gave Joanna medicine. "She is very sick," they said.

The next day, Joanna was still very sick. She lay in bed all the time, not moving. Sometimes her eyes were closed. Sometimes she was looking out the window.

25 The doctors came to see her again.

"Can't you do something?" asked Sue.

"We're doing everything," they said. "But she's still very weak, and she seems sad. Is she unhappy about something?"

"I don't think so," said Sue.

30 But after that, she watched Joanna more closely. Joanna often looked out the window. Sue looked out, too. There was a white wall outside. In front of it was a small tree with just a few yellow leaves. Joanna said something very quietly. Sue moved closer.

"Twelve," said Joanna. A little later she said, "Eleven . . . ten."

"Ten what?" asked Sue.

"Ten leaves . . . on the tree." Sue had to move very close. "Before, there were lots more. Now there are only ten."

Sue didn't like this talk about the leaves. "Do you want a drink of water?" she asked.

"No, no. Look, only eight now. Soon there won't be any. Tonight they'll all go. And I'll go, too."

"Don't talk that way!" said Sue.

Joanna still looked out the window, watching the leaves.

When it was dark, she couldn't see the tree outside. But she lay awake most of the night. Sue was awake, too. Then before it was light, Joanna fell asleep. Sue quietly left the room. When she came back it was already morning. Joanna woke up. She looked out the window. There was one leaf left on the tree.

Sue said nothing.

The doctors came and went. They gave Joanna more medicine and talked with Sue again. "She's not worse, but not better," they said.

All day Sue waited with Joanna. Joanna watched the leaf on the tree. She slept a little. But she did not want to eat or drink, not even a little water. All day she waited for the leaf to fall. In the evening, it was still there. That night it was rainy and windy. No leaf could stay on a tree after a night like that. But in the morning, the tree still had its leaf.

Joanna looked at it a long time. Then she said very quietly to Sue, "Can I have a little water." A little later, she fell asleep and slept for many hours. When she woke, she wanted to sit up a little. She wanted more water and something to eat.

"The worst is over," the doctors said. "Now she just needs to get stronger."

A week later, Joanna left the hospital. Before Sue left Joanna's room, she looked out the window. The last leaf was still on the tree.

It stayed on the tree all winter, all the next year, and for many years after that. Slowly, slowly, it washed off the wall.

(adapted from a story by O. Henry)

Words	Meanings
_____	_____
_____	_____
_____	_____
_____	_____

The Way to a Woman's Heart

Many years ago, Jeff Peters lived in the western United States. He traveled from town to town with a horse and wagon. In each town, he sold things—medicine, soap, shampoo, ribbons. One day he came to a small town in Oklahoma.

5   He went to the only restaurant in town for dinner. On the door, there were lots of signs: "Best Apple Pie in Oklahoma, Fried Chicken Like Your Grandma's, Biggest Steak Around, Pancakes You'll Never Forget!"

"This is just the place for me!" Jeff thought. The cook was an older woman. The waitress was her daughter. She was young and pretty. Jeff smiled and tried
10 to talk with her. But she was in a hurry. There were many hungry people in the restaurant. She didn't even look at him.

The next evening, Jeff was back in the restaurant. He learned that the waitress' name was Mame. He said the food was very good. But again she didn't look at him. Jeff tried going to the restaurant very early or very late,
15 when it wasn't busy. But even then, Mame didn't want to talk to him.

One evening he waited outside the restaurant after a late dinner. When she came out, he asked her to take a walk with him.

"No, thank you," she said.

"But why not?" he said. "Why won't you go out with me?"
20   This time, she looked at him and said, "Every day I see men like you eating. You eat and eat. Food and more food. I can't go out with you! When I see you, I think of food! I'm sick of food!"

After that, Jeff knew he should forget about Mame. But he couldn't. A few days later, it was time for him to move on to another town. On his last evening,
25 he waited at the restaurant for Mame. "I just wanted to say goodbye," he said.

"I'm leaving, too," said Mame. My sister's getting married in Oklahoma City."

"That's where I'm going," said Jeff. "I'll give you a ride."

"No, thanks," said Mame. But her mother said yes. Why not take a free ride? So in the end, she climbed up onto Jeff's wagon. Jeff was very happy with
30 Mame on his wagon. He didn't think much about where he was going, and soon he was lost. It got dark, and it was raining. They were still far from the city. They came to a little house with nobody in it. Jeff made a fire, and he made a bed for Mame with some blankets near the fire. He slept in the other room.

In the morning, they looked out the window. It was raining very hard, and
35 there was water all around the house. They couldn't leave.

Jeff was hungry, but he didn't say anything.

"She hates food," he was thinking. "I can't talk about food."

All day they sat and waited. They talked about lots of things. But they didn't talk about food. In the evening, Jeff made another fire. They were quiet.
40 Jeff was now very hungry. He thought about all the good things he wanted to eat. He tried to think about other things, but he could only think about food.

He closed his eyes. He thought to himself, "Mmmm. My favorite foods. . . . fried eggs over easy, with bacon, toast, and potatoes." But he didn't just think those words. He said them aloud.

45 "With coffee cake and doughnuts," said Mame.

Jeff opened his eyes. "Chicken pie, potatoes, and salad," he said, louder.

"With corn bread and chocolate cake," said Mame.

"Pork roast, rice, and beans," said Jeff.

"With apple sauce and cherry pie," said Mame.

50 Now she was smiling. Jeff began to laugh, and so did Mame. They laughed and talked for hours about food—all their favorite dishes.

The next morning, it wasn't raining, and the water was gone. They left for Oklahoma City. When they got there, they went to a restaurant and asked for all the best dishes.

55 When the food was on the table, Mame said, "Jeff, I guess I was a silly girl. We all need food. We all need to eat. If you want to ask me out again, I won't say no. But let's have dinner now."

So Jeff and Mame went out for a walk after dinner, and a short time later they were married.

(adapted from a story by O. Henry)

Words	**Meanings**

Story 11

The Town That Saved Children

In July, 1942, 40 children arrived in Nonantola, in northern Italy. These children were from Germany and other European countries. Some were young, some were older. They were all Jewish. And they had no families. Their parents were dead—killed by the Nazis in Germany. These children and the teachers
5 with them wanted to go to Palestine (the area where Israel is today). But they couldn't get there because of the war. They lived in Yugoslavia for more than a year. But then the Germans arrived, and the children had to leave. So they went to Italy to wait for the war to end.

In 1942 all Jewish people in Italy had to follow many rules. They couldn't
10 work for non-Jewish people. They couldn't go into non-Jewish stores. They couldn't send their children to Italian schools. They couldn't go out after dark. But they were still safe in Italy. The Italians didn't kill Jewish people.

In Nonantola, the children went to live with their teachers in Villa Emma. Villa Emma was a big and beautiful house, but it was almost empty. There weren't enough tables and chairs for everyone. There weren't enough beds or blankets. There weren't enough plates or cups or spoons. And there were no books, paper, or pencils. School was important for these children and their teachers. Someday they wanted to have a new life in Palestine. They wanted to be ready for that life.

The teachers had some money from an Italian Jewish organization. With that money they could buy food for a few months. But they couldn't buy food for the whole winter. And they couldn't buy everything they needed at the Villa.

Soon after they arrived in Nonantola, they had a visitor. It was Don Arrigo Beccari, a priest from the church in town. He talked with the teachers and the children. He heard about how they left home two years earlier. He heard about the families of the children. He heard that some children cried at night, and that some children were not well. He saw how empty the Villa was.

Don Beccari went back to the town. He talked with his friend, Dr. Moreali, the town doctor. Don Beccari and Dr. Moreali knew everyone in town. And they knew all about their lives and problems. The people of Nonantola liked these two men very much.

The two men talked and talked about the children at Villa Emma. In the next few days, they found answers to many of the problems. Don Beccari found some beds, chairs, and tables at a Catholic school. Soon a truck brought them to Villa Emma. Dr. Moreali went to see the sick children and gave them some medicine. Soon they were better. Don Beccari talked with some farmers. Soon the older boys and girls were working on farms. The farmers paid them with potatoes, eggs, or chickens. In this way, they had food for the winter.

The fall and then the winter came to Villa Emma. Everyone in Nonantola knew about the children. Many people helped. They gave Don Beccari food, clothes, or toys to bring to the Villa. With help from the town, there was enough food all winter. There was also wood to keep the Villa warm.

In the spring, another group of Jewish children arrived. Now there were 73 children and their teachers. The older boys and girls began to work on the farms again. In the summer, when it was hot, the children went swimming. There was a big river near Villa Emma. This was also a good place for meetings in the long summer evenings. Young people from the town met with young people from the Villa. Some became good friends, and some fell in love. But the young people had to hide their meetings. They were afraid of the Italian police.

Did the police in Nonantola know about Villa Emma? Did they know that the young Jews worked on Italian farms? Did they know that many Nonantolans met with the Jewish children and teachers? Did they know that Don Beccari and Dr. Moreali and many people in town were helping them? They almost certainly knew. But they did nothing. They said nothing to Don Beccari and Dr. Moreali. They said nothing to other people in town.

And then, suddenly, everything changed. In early September, 1943, the German army arrived in northern Italy. Now it was not a safe place for Jewish people. The German soldiers told the Italians to find all the Jews and send them to Germany. Everyone knew what happened to Jews who were sent to the Nazi camps. They were killed in terrible ways.

In many towns, the Italians helped the Germans find all the Jewish people. But the people of Nonantola didn't. They wanted to save the children and teachers of Villa Emma. So they took them into their homes and hid them. In two days, Villa Emma was empty. All the children and their teachers were hiding with families in the town or in a Catholic school.

Now the German soldiers were in Nonantola. Everyone was afraid. The children and teachers were safe for the moment, but not for long. Everyone in Nonantola knew about Villa Emma. The police in Nonantola knew, too. In those first days, they kept the secret. They didn't tell the German soldiers about the Jews. But they couldn't keep the secret for much longer.

Don Beccari and Dr. Moreali talked about this terrible new problem. They had to find a way to get all the children and teachers out of Italy. The only safe country now was Switzerland. But Switzerland was not close to Nonantola. It was several hours away.

With the help of many people from Nonantola, they made a plan. It was very dangerous—for the Jews and for their helpers. A man who worked in the town hall made ID papers for the children and teachers. These papers didn't say they were Jewish. They said the children belonged to a school and were on a school trip.

Then the children and teachers began leaving in small groups. They went first by truck and then by train. Then they had to walk for miles. Finally, at night, they came to a river. It was wide and deep, but on the other side was Switzerland. The older children held the hands of the younger children. Night by night, and group by group, they all made the trip across the river.

Only one child was not saved this way. This boy was not at Villa Emma when the Germans arrived. He was sick in the hospital. There the Germans found him. They sent him with other Jews to Germany, where he died. Later, one of the helpers from Nonantola also died. He was helping another group of Jews leave Italy, and the German soldiers caught him.

All the other children from Villa Emma lived in Switzerland until the end of the war. Then at last, in 1945, they went to Palestine.

(a true story)

Words	**Meanings**
_____	_____
_____	_____
_____	_____
_____	_____

Who Took the Money?

Manuel lived in a village in Spain called San José. It was a small village in the mountains. When he was 15, Manuel started working on the Spanish trains. Every Monday morning, he went by train down to the city. He came back home again on Friday evening. He worked long hours, and he worked
5   very hard.

When he was 24, he married Maria. She was from the next village. They had two daughters, Sofia and Lucinda. Manuel didn't see his family very much. He was away at work five days a week. But he had a good job, and that was important.

10   Santa Maria was a poor village. Many men there didn't have good jobs. They worked only for a few months every year. Their families did not have money for meat or coffee. Their children did not have good coats or shoes. But Manuel's daughters always had good coats and shoes. The family had meat, coffee, and many good things to eat. On Sundays Sofia and Lucinda had ice
15   cream after dinner.

But not all of Manuel's money went to his family. Every month, he put a little money in the bank. He didn't tell Maria about this. "A little money in the bank is important," he thought. "But money can be a bad thing. People can get angry and fight about it. I'm not going to tell Maria or the girls about this. Not
20   now. Someday I'll tell them, and we'll do something special. We'll all go stay in a hotel by the sea."

Year after year, Manuel put a little money in the bank. His daughters got married and moved to the city. Sofia married Ruiz, and they had two children, a boy and a girl. Lucinda married Carlos, and they had a girl. On weekends
25   Sofia and Lucinda often went back to the village with their children. The children liked the village, and they loved their grandparents. They played in the garden with the dog and the cat. They went up the mountain with Manuel to get flowers and fruit. Maria cooked big meals for them and made them warm clothes.

30   When Manuel was 65, he stopped working. Now he didn't go to the city every week. He stayed in the village with his wife. He worked in the garden, and he took care of his fruit trees. He walked a lot in the mountains, and sometimes he sat with his friends in the café. They drank coffee, talked, and played cards. He still got money every month from the government, and he
35   still put a little money in the bank.

"Soon I'll tell Maria and the girls about my money," he thought. "And next summer, we'll all go to the seaside."

But Manuel and Maria always had lots of things to do. They had the house and the garden, the dog and the cat, and the grandchildren. The grandchildren went to school in the city now. But sometimes they were sick, and sometimes there was no school. Then they stayed with Manuel and Maria.

One day Maria didn't feel very well. She went to bed, and Manuel called the doctor. The doctor said it was nothing. But after a week, Maria still didn't feel well. The doctor sent her to the hospital in the city. The hospital doctors did lots of tests. They told the family she was very sick. Manuel, Lucinda, and Sofia stayed with her night and day in the hospital. A month went by, and Maria didn't get better. The doctors then said she was going to die.

Sofia and Lucinda drove her home to the village. She lived for a few more months. Manuel stayed with her all the time. The daughters came often. And then, one day, she said goodbye to Manuel, and she died.

Lucinda and Sofia stayed with Manuel for a week after that. They put away all Maria's clothes and things. They cleaned the house and cooked. Then they went back to the city, back to their families and their jobs.

Now Manuel was alone. Some women in the village said, "We can help you in the house. We can make dinner for you and wash your clothes. You don't have to pay us very much."

But Manuel didn't want other women in his house. He also didn't want to pay these women. He had money in the bank, but it was for his family.

Some years went by. Manuel learned how to cook and how to wash his clothes. His house was always clean, and his garden was full of fruit and vegetables. Now his grandchildren were older. They didn't come very often because they had to study on the weekends. His daughters said, "Why don't you come live in the city with us?"

But Manuel didn't want to leave his home. He was 77 years old. On some days, he felt very old and tired. Then he liked to sit in his garden with his cat and his dog. Of course, they weren't the same cat and dog. They were the grandchildren of the first cat and dog.

One day Manuel looked at the cat and the dog. Now they were old, too. The dog never barked, and the cat never ran after mice. "We're all old now," Manuel said to them. "We're all going to die before long. Then who will get my money? I don't want the bank to have it! I must go and get it."

So, one morning, Manuel went to the bank. He asked for all his money. The bank manager came and talked to Manuel. He said, "What are you going to do with all this money? You have 30,000 euros. You can't walk home with 30,000 euros!"

Manuel just said, "It's my money. I can do what I want with it." He put the money in a big bag, and he carried it home. At home, he put the money under his bed. But that night he didn't sleep well. When the cat came into his room, he said, "Who's that?!" and jumped out of bed.

(continued)

80 In the morning, he went out to the garden. He made a big hole under a plum tree. He put the bag of money in the hole. He put dirt back in the hole, and he put grass on top. Every day he looked at that place under the plum tree. He often thought about the money. But it stayed under the plum tree. He couldn't decide what to do with it. He could give 15,000 euros to each
85 daughter. But Sofia had two children and Lucinda had only one. So that was not good. He could give money only to the grandchildren—10,000 each. But that meant no money for his daughters. He couldn't do that.

While Manuel thought about his money, the winter went by. Spring came, and there were lots of flowers on the plum tree. Then summer came, and
90 Manuel's garden was full of fruit and vegetables once again. But the plum tree had very few plums, and those plums were not sweet.

"I think the tree is telling me something," said Manuel. "Money shouldn't stay in a hole in the ground."

He telephoned his daughters. "Please come this weekend," he said. "I have
95 something important to tell you."

Sofia and Lucinda came on Friday evening with their husbands and their children. Sofia's daughter, Yolanda, was now 20 years old, and her son, Pablo, was 17. Yolanda was a university student. She was studying to be a doctor. Pablo was a high school student, like Lucinda's daughter, Julia.

100 At dinner that evening, Manuel said nothing about the money. Lucinda looked at Sofia, and Sofia looked at her father. But he didn't say anything important. They talked about the city and the government. They talked about the village and the garden. Yolanda, Pablo, and Julia went for a walk around the village. "What's he going to tell us?" they asked. But Manuel told them
105 nothing that evening, and they all went to bed.

At breakfast the next morning, Manuel said, "Today's the day. Now I'm ready. Come with me to the garden."

Manuel went to the plum tree and stopped. "I'm getting old," he said. "I'm going to die before long. I want to give you something."

110 He took the grass away from the hole, and he took out the dirt. "Oh, no!" he cried.

"What is it?" asked his daughters.

"Look!" he said. "Look at that hole. It's empty!" Manuel sat down in the grass. "Who took it?" he cried. "Who took it?"

115 "Who took what?" asked Sofia and Lucinda.

"My money!" said Manuel.

"Your money?" they asked. "Why did you put money in the ground? Money should be in the bank."

"I didn't want the bank to have my money. It was my money," said Manuel.
120 "I wanted to give it to you."

"How much was it?" asked Sofia.

"Thirty thousand euros," said Manuel.

"Thirty thousand!" cried Sofia and Lucinda. "You put all that money in a hole in the ground?"

125   Poor Manuel. He sat on the ground with his head in his hands.

"We must go to the police!" said Ruiz.

"Yes, we must tell them," said Carlos. "Maybe they can find the thief."

So Ruiz, Carlos, Sofia, and Lucinda ran to the police. Yolanda, Pablo, and Julia stayed with Manuel in the garden. Julia looked in the hole. She put her
130 hands in and pulled out some very small pieces of paper.

"Look!" she said. "Look at these."

"Pieces of money!" said Pablo.

"Why is it in little pieces?" asked Yolanda. "What kind of thief does that?"

"It looks like there were many small thieves," said Julia.
135 "Children!" said Yolanda. "That's terrible! Village children!"

"No, not children," said Julia. "Very, very small thieves. They ate the money."

"What do you mean?" asked Pablo.

"Look in the hole," said Julia. "Do you see those little black things? What makes little black things? What eats paper?"
140 "Mice!!!" cried Pablo and Yolanda.

"Yes, mice," said Julia.

Manuel looked up. "It's true," he said. "There are lots of mice. The cat is old, and she doesn't run after them now." He looked at Yolanda, Pablo, and Julia. "I'm very sorry," he said. "I wanted to give you that money. I wanted to
145 send you to the seaside. I wanted . . ." He stopped.

The cat came out and sat down near Manuel. She was black and white and very fat.

"Where were you?" said Julia to the cat. "Why weren't you out here at work?"
150 "Meow!" said the cat.

Then Pablo started to laugh. "Think about it," he said. "Thirty thousand! Those mice ate thirty thousand euros!"

Yolanda and Julia started to laugh, too.

"What are the police going to do?" said Pablo. "Put the mice in jail?"
155 Yolanda, Pablo, and Julia laughed more and more. They fell on the ground laughing.

Manuel looked at them, and he thought, "How can they laugh? That was years of work, that money."

He listened to his grandchildren, still laughing and talking. And then he
160 thought, "Maybe they're right. Why cry? I can't get the money back now." And he smiled sadly at the cat.

(fiction)

Words	**Meanings**
_____	_____
_____	_____
_____	_____
_____	_____

Choosing a Book

You should look for books for learners of English. Look for beginning level books: Level 1 or Stage 1. Ask your teacher where to find books for your level. There may be some in the school or classroom library. You may also find books for learners in bookstores or public libraries.

Choose a book that interests you. Your teacher and friends may have good ideas. The important thing is to choose a book that *you* want to read.

At the end of this unit, there is a list of books. You may choose from these books, or you may choose different books.

Before you choose a book, find out if it's right for you. Follow these steps to preview it:

- Read the title, back cover, and first page. What is the book about? Is it interesting?
- Look at the first page again. How many words are new for you?
    No new words   This book may be *too easy* for you.
    1–5 new words   This book is *the right level* for you.
    6 or more new words   This book may be *too difficult* for you.

EXAMPLE

A. *Look at the example on page 49. Then answer these questions.*

   1. What is the title? _The Big Bag Mistake_____

   2. Look at the front cover and read the back cover copy. Then read the first page.

      What is this book about? _____

      Is it interesting to you? _____

   3. Look at the first page again.

      How many words are new for you? _____

      Is this book the right level for you? _____

B. *Talk about your answers with another student. Are they the same?*

PENGUIN READERS

The Big Bag Mistake

John Escott

(from the back cover)

Ricardo and Gisela are going home to Rio. Gisela likes reading and quiet people. Ricardo likes noise . . . and he likes Gisela. In Rio, a thief takes Gisesla's bag. What can Ricardo do?

Gisela is going home to Rio de Janeiro after a month's vacation in London. She lives in an apartment in Rio with two friends.

Her airplane leaves at five o'clock. It is one o'clock now. Gisela puts her clothes and a manuscript into a travel bag. This manuscript is very important to her. She is writing her first book.

1

Learning New Words from Your Books

Don't stop every time you find a new word. Continue reading. Then try to guess the meaning or try to understand the story without it.

When you finish a book (or a chapter), go back and look for new words.

1. Underline the new words.
2. Try to guess the meanings.
3. Check the meanings in the dictionary.
4. Write the words and the meanings in your vocabulary notebook.

manuscript (noun)	*a book or piece of*
Gisela puts her	*writing before*
clothes and a	*it is printed*
manuscript into	
a travel bag.	

Talking about Your Books

Book Conferences

A book conference is a conversation with your teacher. It is not a test. Tell your teacher when you finish a book. Then your teacher will talk with you about it.

You don't need to study for a book conference. You just need to read the book!

Here are some questions your teacher may ask:
- What is the title?
- Who is the author (writer)?
- Where does the story take place?
- Who is it about?
- What happens to them?
- Did you like the book? Why or why not?

Reading Circles

A reading circle is a small group of students. They meet often to talk about the books they are reading.

Rules for Reading Circles

- The group should have four to five students.
- One student starts. This student tells about his/her book (not more than four minutes).
- Use these guidelines for talking about your book:
    1. Where are you in the book? (beginning, middle, end)
    2. Who is it about?
    3. Where are they?
    4. What happens to them?
    5. Is the book easy or difficult?
    6. Do you like it? Why or why not?
- One by one, the other students tell about their books (not more than four minutes each).
- Students who are not talking must listen and then ask questions. They also watch the time. They say when four minutes have passed.

Book Talks

In a book talk, you talk to the class about your book. You should only talk for a few minutes (not more than five minutes).

How to Get Ready for Book Talks

- Write the answers to these questions on a small piece of paper. Don't write whole sentences. Write only a few notes (words or phrases) for each answer.
    1. What is the title?
    2. Who is the author?
    3. Is it easy or difficult?
    4. Who is it about?
    5. Where are they?
    6. What happens to them?
    7. Did you like the book? Why or why not?
- Use your answers to these questions to talk about the book.
- Practice your talk before you give it in class. Try not to read your notes. Look up. Speak slowly and loudly.
- When you practice, time your talk. If it takes less than four minutes, think of more things to say. If it takes more than five minutes, cut out some parts.

Writing about Your Books

Book Reports

When you finish a book, ask your teacher for a book report form. Answer the questions about your book. Then give the form to your teacher.

BOOK REPORT

Title: _____

Author: _____

Number of pages: _____   Fiction or nonfiction: _____

Was the book easy or difficult for you?

_____

Who is it about? _____

Where are they? _____

What happens to them? (Tell only the most important things.)

_____

_____

_____

_____

What did you like about the book?

_____

_____

What didn't you like about it?

_____

_____

Rate this book: _____

★★★★ = a great book!	★ = not very interesting
★★★ = a good book	✗ = a terrible book
★★ = some good parts	

Book Files

When you finish a book, ask your teacher for a book file card. Then make a card for your class book files. You and your classmates can use the files to find books you like.

On the card, write information about your book. Follow the example below. Remember to rate your book.

★ ★ ★ ★ = a great book!
★ ★ ★ = a good book
★ ★ = some good parts
★ = not very interesting
✗ = a terrible book

EXAMPLE

TITLE: *The Big Bag Mistake*

AUTHOR: *John Escott*

NUMBER OF PAGES: *15*   **FICTION OR NONFICTION:** *Fiction*

WHAT IS THE BOOK ABOUT? *It's a very funny story. It's about a man named Ricardo and a woman named Gisela. They are going to Rio, but Gisela has a problem with her bag.*

RATE THE BOOK: ☆ ☆ ☆

Reading List

Make a list of your extensive reading books here. For each book you read, write the title, author, and the date you finished.

1. Title: _____

   Author: _____   Date finished: _____

2. Title: _____

   Author: _____   Date finished: _____

(continued)

3. Title: _____

   Author: _____   Date finished: _____

4. Title: _____

   Author: _____   Date finished: _____

5. Title: _____

   Author: _____   Date finished: _____

6. Title: _____

   Author: _____   Date finished: _____

7. Title: _____

   Author: _____   Date finished: _____

8. Title: _____

   Author: _____   Date finished: _____

9. Title: _____

   Author: _____   Date finished: _____

10. Title: _____

    Author: _____   Date finished: _____

11. Title: _____

    Author: _____   Date finished: _____

12. Title: _____

    Author: _____   Date finished: _____

Book List

The books on this list are all published by Penguin Longman. Other companies also have books for English learners. The books with a headphones symbol (🎧) have an audio CD. Listening and reading at the same time is very good practice. If you listen and read the first time, you can try just reading or just listening another time.

Beginning Level

Longman Easy Starts

April in Moscow. Rabley, Stephen. April is a dancer. When she goes to Moscow, she meets a young man named Nicolai. She thinks she may never see him again.

Between Two Worlds. Rabley, Stephen. Joanna is a nurse in Australia. She works with a Flying Doctor. One day Joanna goes to Sydney with a sick baby.

The Big Bag Mistake. Escott, John. Ricardo and Gisela are going home to Rio de Janeiro. In Rio, a thief takes Gisela's bag. Ricardo must find the thief.

Billy and the Queen. Rabley, Stephen. Billy and his sister want new bicycles, but they don't have the money. Then they find a way to win some money.

Dino's Day in London. Rabley, Stephen. Tommy Grant is a taxi driver. One day he is a driver for Dino, the son of a film star.

Fireboy. Rabley, Stephen. Hapu lives in ancient Egypt. His father is ill and he needs money for the doctor. Hapu thinks Queen Cleopatra will help him.

Flying Home. Rabley, Stephen. Felix is not a happy bird. He comes from Brazil, but now he lives in New York. One day his cage opens, and he says goodbye to New York.

Hannah and the Hurricane. Escott, John. Hannah takes people out on a boat every day. She loves her job. A rich man arrives with a big new boat. But then there is a hurricane.

The Last Photo. Smith, Bernard. Pam and Martin are visiting Cambridge. They take some photos. In one of the photos, there is a man. The police are looking for this man.

The Leopard and the Lighthouse. Collins, Anne. One day a leopard swims across the sea to Sindi. He goes into a lighthouse. What should the people of Sindi do?

Lucky Break. Escott, John. Tom breaks his leg in a football game. Then he sees his favorite movie star. Suddenly he is falling again and the movie star is falling, too.

Maisie and the Dolphin. Rabley, Stephen. Maisie lives in the Bahamas. She makes friends with a dolphin named Ben and helps him get well. Then Maisie needs help.

Marcel and the Mona Lisa. Rabley, Stephen. Marcel is a French mouse and a detective. One evening he sees a man steal a famous painting from the Louvre.

Marcel and the White Star. Rabley, Stephen. Marcel, the French detective mouse, lives in Paris. One evening two thieves steal a very expensive diamond ring.

New Zealand Adventure. Thorburn, Jan. Sarah and Jessica arrive in New Zealand for a holiday. They find a telephone in the taxi from the airport.

Simon and the Spy. Laird, Elizabeth. Simon goes on a vacation. On the train, he meets Samantha. He likes her, and she likes him. They don't see the spy.

The Pearl Girl. Rabley, Stephen. Kate comes from Canada. She is visiting Europe with her parents. One evening she sees two men with a famous picture.

Tinker's Farm. Rabley, Stephen. In 1800, Jenny Tinker arrives in New York with her father. They want to start a new life in America. How can they get money for a farm?

Tinker's Island. Rabley, Stephen. In 1798, Jenny Tinker and her father live in London. One day a man steals a watch. The policemen think it was Jenny's father.

Tom Cruise. Smith, Rod. Tom Cruise is one of Hollywood's most famous actors. Read about his life and his work in films.

The Troy Stone. Rabley, Stephen. Mark is on vacation in Turkey. He visits the old city of Troy and finds a yellow stone. Suddenly he goes back in time.

The White Oryx. Smith, Bernard. Mandy is in the desert with Abdullah. The oryx is a very special animal, and there are only a few of them. Then they find a dead mother oryx.

Who Wants to Be a Star? Allen, Julia; Iggulden, Margaret. Tina is 13 years old and a star. She sings beautifully, and her mother has big ideas about Hollywood. But Tina is not happy.

Penguin Active Reading Easy Starts

🎧 *The Blue Cat Club.* Smith, Bernard. James and Chantal are at the Blue Cat Club. Merlin the magician is doing some tricks. But these tricks may be dangerous.

🎧 *Kim's Choice.* Viney, Brigit. Kim loves running, and she's very fast. She wins more and more prizes. But then she has to make a difficult choice.

🎧 *The Long Road.* Smith, Rod. Terry Fox has cancer and an artificial leg. He runs all the way across Canada to help sick children. This is the story of a strong athlete and a Canadian hero.

🎧 *The Newspaper Chase.* Escott, John. Harry Black steals a million-dollar picture. He hides it in some newspapers. But someone finds those newspapers and wants to recycle them.

Elementary Level

Penguin Readers Level 1

🎧 *20,000 Leagues Under the Sea.* Verne, Jules. This is the story of Captain Nemo and his submarine, the Nautilus. He finds three men in the sea and a beautiful town under water.

🎧 *The Adventures of Tom Sawyer.* Twain, Mark. Tom Sawyer loves adventures. He has them at home, at school, and with his friends Becky Thatcher and Huckleberry Finn.

Ali and His Camera. Pizante, Raymond. Ali wants to take pictures of people and places in Istanbul. But how can he get a camera?

The Battle of Newton Road. Dunkling, Leslie. The houses on Newton Road are small, but people are happy there. Then someone wants to knock down the houses and build a road.

Daniel Radcliffe. Shipton, Vicky. His face is famous from the Harry Potter movies. But what did he do before Harry Potter? And how did he get the job?

David Beckham. Smith, Bernard. David Beckham played soccer for England and for Manchester United. How did he start to play soccer? Why is he so famous?

The Gift of the Magi & Other Stories. O. Henry. Famous stories by O. Henry. He writes about New York, Texas, and Oklahoma. There is always a surprise.

Girl Meets Boy. Strange, Derek. A girl meets a boy on the boat to Spain. She wants to see him again, but there are problems.

The House of the Seven Gables. Hawthorne, Nathaniel. The house is the home of an important family. They have the house and a lot of land, but no money and many problems.

Jennifer Lopez. Smith, Rod. Jennifer Lopez is a Hollywood star and a famous singer. She is a Latin performer, and her life is fun and exciting.

Karen and the Artist. Laird, Elizabeth. Karen's job takes her to many places. In Rome, she meets a young artist and wants to help him sell his pictures.

Lisa in London. Victor, Paul. It is Lisa's first visit to London. She is learning English. Then she meets Michael.

Marcel and the Shakespeare Letters. Rabley, Stephen. Marcel, the French mouse detective, helps his friend Henry look for some letters by William Shakespeare.

Marcel goes to Hollywood. Rabley, Stephen. Marcel, the French mouse detective, goes to Los Angeles on holiday. Then a girl is kidnapped.

Michael Jordan. Taylor, Nancy. Michael Jordan may be the best basketball player of all time. Where did he come from? How did he start in basketball?

Mike's Lucky Day. Dunkling, Leslie. Mike drives a van. He meets Jennifer in her father's shop. They are going to the cinema together. But Mike is very late.

The Missing Coins. Escott, John. Pete and Carla are students. One day, they look at some coins in a shop. Later that day, some of the coins are missing.

Mother Teresa. Adrian-Vallance, D'Arcy. Mother Teresa was small and quiet. She helped poor people on the streets in India. Why do people remember her and love her today?

🎧 *Muhammed Ali.* Smith, Bernard. In 1974, Muhammed Ali became the boxing champion of the world. How did this boy from Kentucky become a champion?

Pelé. Smith, Rod. Pelé is the number one player in the history of soccer. He won the World Cup three times for Brazil. This is his story.

🎧 *Rip Van Winkle & The Legend of Sleepy Hollow.* Irving, Washington. Rip Van Winkle walks into the mountains one day and meets some strange old men. He comes back twenty years later.

Run for Your Life. Waller, Stephen. Kim is running through the streets of Barcelona. A man with dark eyes and a knife is looking for her.

Six Sketches. Dunkling, Leslie. Norma is always right. But there are lots of questions she needs to answer. The answers are in these six sketches.

Surfer! Harvey, Paul. Nick wants to win a surfing competition and go to Australia. But his father is not happy.

Penguin Active Reading Level 1

🎧 *Amazon Rally.* Amos, Eduardo. Brian and David ride in a motorcycle race through the forest in Brazil. Then they meet some Indians.

🎧 *Island for Sale.* Collins, Anne. Duncan lives in a castle on an island in Scotland. But he doesn't have any money so he decides to sell the island.

Kylie Minogue. Kilbey, Liz. Kylie was a rich and famous singer. Then she got cancer. But she came back and began singing again.

🎧 *Little Women.* Alcott, Louisa May. This is the famous story of the four March sisters and their relationships, problems, and adventures.

PART

2

Vocabulary Building

Guidelines for Learning Vocabulary

To be a good reader, you need to know many words. How can you learn more words?

Follow these guidelines for learning vocabulary:

1. ***Make good use of the dictionary.***
   - Learn the pronunciation, spelling, and part of speech of new words.
   - Find the best meaning and learn how to use each word.

2. ***Study vocabulary often.***
   - Use a vocabulary notebook and study cards to help you learn and review new words.

> ***Note:*** Ask your teacher which language to use when you write the meanings of words. Should you write them in English or in your language?

Make Good Use of the Dictionary

Choosing a Good Dictionary

You will need a dictionary for the exercises in this unit (and for other vocabulary work). Check with your teacher about which is the best dictionary for you.

If possible, use an English learner's dictionary. For example, the *Longman Study Dictionary* is a good dictionary for this level. Learner's dictionaries are easier to use than other English dictionaries. The meanings are written in simple English. They also have information about words and how they are used.

You may also use a bilingual dictionary in your language. These dictionaries may give less information about how to use the words in English.

Pronunciation

It is important to learn how to pronounce (say) words. Saying words aloud helps you remember them. In fact, if you can't say a word, it's very hard to remember it.

Most dictionaries tell you how to pronounce words. They use special pronunciation symbols (letters). Look in your dictionary for the key to these symbols. (It's often on the inside back cover.)

EXERCISE 1

A. **Work with another student. Find the pronunciation key in your dictionary. Take turns saying the example words for each symbol.**

B. **Read the words and the pronunciation symbols below. Say the words to your partner.**

1. a. buy /baɪ/   b. fly /flaɪ/   c. child /tʃaɪld/
2. a. date /deɪt/   b. wait /weɪt/   c. break /breɪk/
3. a. feel /fil/   b. mean /min/   c. piece /pis/

C. **Say the words again for your teacher.**

EXERCISE 2

A. **Follow these steps for each group of words.**

1. **Read a line of words aloud to another student.**

2. **Look up each word in the dictionary. Check the pronunciation symbols. Did you say the words correctly?**

3. **Practice saying the words correctly.**

4. **Listen to another student read a line of words to you. Then check the pronunciation and practice the words.**

1. a. late   b. hair   c. can   d. walk
2. a. fell   b. few   c. she   d. pretty
3. a. ill   b. machine   c. dirt   d. dining room
4. a. earth   b. great   c. ocean   d. meal
5. a. die   b. field   c. friend   d. quiet
6. a. book   b. moon   c. poor   d. stood
7. a. bought   b. country   c. through   d. amount
8. a. danger   b. dog   c. bring   d. right

B. *Say the words again for your teacher.*

C. *Talk about these questions with another student.*

- What can you say about spelling and pronunciation in English?
- What can you say about spelling and pronunciation in your language?

Remember

When you look up a new word, check the pronunciation.
A letter (or group of letters) may be pronounced in many different ways.

Examples: blood /ʌ/, boot /u/, hood /ʊ/

Different letters (or groups of letters) may have the same pronunciation.

Examples: beach, piece, feet /i/, country, blood, under /ʌ/

Spelling

It's important to know how to spell words in English. If you know the spelling of a word, you know what it looks like. Then you can read it more quickly.

When you learn new words, you should also learn the spelling.

EXERCISE 3

A. *Your teacher will read some words to you (from Exercise 2, column a). Listen and write the words. Don't look back at Exercise 2.*

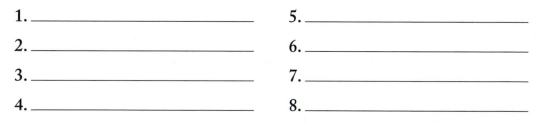

1. _____   5. _____

2. _____   6. _____

3. _____   7. _____

4. _____   8. _____

B. *Now look back at the words in Exercise 2, column a. Did you spell them correctly? Correct them if necessary.*

C. *Work in pairs. Student A, read the "b" words from Exercise 2 to your partner. Student B, listen and write the words. Don't look at Exercise 2. Then change roles. Student B, read the "c" words.*

D. *Look back at Exercise 2. Did you spell all the words correctly?*

Parts of Speech

The dictionary tells you the part of speech for every word. This helps you understand the word and use it correctly.

Noun (n):	a person, place, thing, quality, or idea
Examples:	I hurt my **finger**.
	She found **happiness** with **Max**.
Verb (v):	a word (words) that shows an action, experience, or state
Examples:	He **ran** all the way home.
	He **likes** ice cream. He **is eating** an ice-cream cone.
Pronoun (pron):	a word that is used instead of a noun or noun phrase
Examples:	**I** will call **him** later.
	They sold **us** a car **that** didn't go.
Adjective (adj):	a word that describes a noun
Examples:	The grass is very **green**.
	Young people often listen to **loud** music.
Adverb (adv):	a word that tells you more about a verb, an adjective, or another adverb
Examples:	I want to see that movie **again**.
	The boy was **very** unhappy. He began to cry **loudly**.
Preposition (prep):	a word that is put in front of a noun to show where, when, or how
Examples:	He came **to** the party **with** his girlfriend.
	My parents live **near** an airport.
Conjunction (conj):	a word that connects sentences or parts of sentences (phrases)
Examples:	He got up **and** had breakfast.
	I was hungry, **so** I ate some crackers.

A. *Find these words on the dictionary page. Write the parts of speech.*

1. direction   _____*noun*_____
2. directness   _____
3. direct   _____

4. directly   _____
5. directions   _____
6. director   _____

B. *Talk about your answers with another student. Are they the same?*

direct[1] /də'rekt/ *adjective*
1 going straight from one place to another:
What's the most direct route to the airport?
2 with no other person, thing, or event involved:
The case was solved as a direct result of her phone call to police. ANTONYM
indirect
3 saying exactly what you mean in an honest and clear way: *She's always very direct, so you don't have to guess what she's thinking.* ANTONYM
indirect
–directness *noun* the quality that a direct person has
direct[2] *verb*
1 to tell the actors what to do in a movie or play:
The movie was directed by Joel Coen.
2 *formal* to tell someone the way to a place: *He directed me to the airport.*
3 to aim something at a particular place, person, etc.: *A lot of advertising is directed at children.*

direction /də'rekʃn/ *noun*
the way that someone or something is moving or pointing: *I think we're going in the wrong direction—we should be heading north.* | *He walked in the direction of the house* (= toward the house).
directions /də'rekʃnz/ *plural noun*
information about how to get to a place or about how to do something: *Could you give me directions to the airport?* | *Follow the directions on the bottle* (= do what they tell you to do).
directly /də'rektli/ *adverb*
1 with no other person, thing, or event involved:
He was driving the car that hit the boys; he is directly responsible for the accident.
2 exactly in a particular position or direction:
Lucas sat directly behind us.
director /də'rektɚ/ *noun*
1 the person who tells the actors what to do in a movie or play
2 someone who controls an organization or one of its activities: *The director of the museum is in charge of all the employees.*

A. *Find these words on the dictionary page. Write the parts of speech.*

1. underline _____*verb*_____
2. underneath _____
3. underground _____
4. undermine _____
5. undergraduate _____
6. undergo _____
7. underlying _____
8. underhand _____

B. *Talk about your answers with another student. Are they the same?*

---

undergo /ˌʌndɚˈgoʊ/ *verb*
underwent /ˌʌndɚˈwɛnt/ **undergone** /ˌʌndɚˈgɔn/
to experience a change or something bad or difficult: *He underwent surgery to remove the cancer.*

undergraduate /ˌʌndɚˈgrædʒuət/ *noun*
a student in college, who is working for his or her Bachelor's Degree: *She's an undergraduate at Notre Dame University.*
–undergraduate adjective relating to undergraduates and the work they do; *undergraduate classes*

underground /ˌʌndɚˈgraʊnd/ *adjective, adverb*
under the earth's surface: *An underground tunnel connects the two buildings.* | *They bury the waste underground.*

undergrowth /ˈʌndɚˌgroʊθ/ *noun*
bushes, small trees, etc. that grow around and under bigger trees: *I couldn't push my way through the dense undergrowth.*

underhand /ˈʌndɚˌhænd/ *adjective, adverb*
thrown with your arm under the level of your shoulder: *The ball will be easier for me to catch if you throw it underhand.*

underline /ˈʌndɚˌlaɪn/ *verb*
to draw a line under a word: *She underlined the important sentences on the page.*

underlying /ˈʌndɚˌlaɪ-ɪŋ/ *adjective, formal*
relating to something that is most important but that is often not easy to notice: *Stress is the underlying cause of the illness.*

undermine /ˈʌndɚˌmaɪn/ *verb*
to do or say something that makes someone or something less strong or effective over a period of time: *All the bad stories about Wilson undermined people's respect for him.*

underneath /ˌʌndɚˈniθ/ *preposition, adverb*
directly below or under something: *He stood underneath the bridge to get out of the rain.* | *We turned some rocks over to see what was underneath.*

Different Meanings

Many words have more than one meaning.

Look at the examples of the word *free* on the dictionary page.

When the different meanings are <u>different</u> parts of speech, there are separate headings.

When the different meanings are the <u>same</u> part of speech, the meanings are numbered. The first meaning is the one used most often.

To find the best meaning for the word as it is used in a sentence, follow these steps:

- Read the sentence. What part of speech is the word? Find the heading for that part of speech.
- If there is more than one meaning under that heading, read the sentence again. Find the best meaning for the sentence.

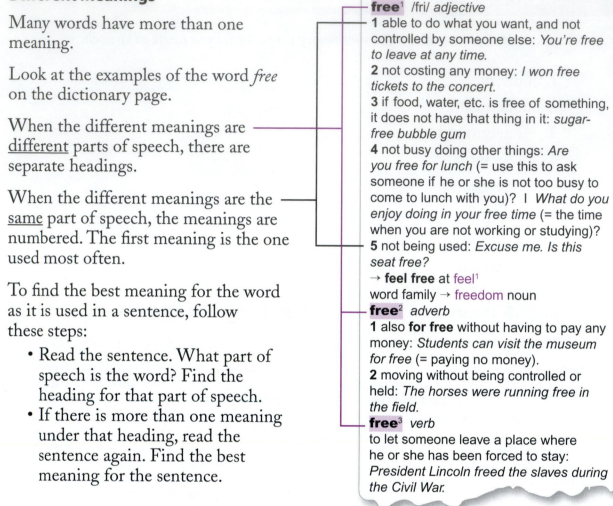

free[1] /frī/ *adjective*
1 able to do what you want, and not controlled by someone else: *You're free to leave at any time.*
2 not costing any money: *I won free tickets to the concert.*
3 if food, water, etc. is free of something, it does not have that thing in it: *sugar-free bubble gum*
4 not busy doing other things: *Are you free for lunch* (= use this to ask someone if he or she is not too busy to come to lunch with you)? | *What do you enjoy doing in your free time* (= the time when you are not working or studying)?
5 not being used: *Excuse me. Is this seat free?*
→ **feel free** at feel[1]
word family → freedom *noun*
free[2] *adverb*
1 also **for free** without having to pay any money: *Students can visit the museum for free* (= paying no money).
2 moving without being controlled or held: *The horses were running free in the field.*
free[3] *verb*
to let someone leave a place where he or she has been forced to stay: *President Lincoln freed the slaves during the Civil War.*

EXAMPLE

Find each underlined word on the dictionary page above. Write the part of speech and the meaning of the word in the sentence.

1. Are you <u>free</u> tomorrow evening? I'd like to go see the new George Clooney movie.

   Part of speech: ___*adjective*___
   Meaning: ___*not busy doing other things*___

2. The army will <u>free</u> the enemy soldiers after the war.

   Part of speech: ___*verb*___
   Meaning: ___*to let someone leave a place where he or she has been forced to stay*___

A. *Find each underlined word on the dictionary page. Write the part of speech and the meaning of the word in the sentence.*

1. He went home by the most <u>direct</u> way.

   Part of speech: _____

   Meaning: _____

   _____

2. You should speak <u>directly</u> with the manager about this.

   Part of speech: _____

   Meaning: _____

   _____

3. We watched an old movie <u>directed</u> by Fellini.

   Part of speech: _____

   Meaning: _____

   _____

4. Marjorie was usually very <u>direct</u>. But this time, she didn't tell us her ideas.

   Part of speech: _____

   Meaning: _____

   _____

B. *Talk about your answers with another student. Are they the same?*

---

direct¹ /dəˈrekt/ *adjective*
1 going straight from one place to another: *What's the most direct route to the airport?*
2 with no other person, thing, or event involved: *The case was solved as a direct result of her phone call to police.* ANTONYM **indirect**
3 saying exactly what you mean in an honest and clear way: *She's always very direct, so you don't have to guess what she's thinking.* ANTONYM **indirect**
—**directness** *noun* the quality that a direct person has

direct² *verb*
1 to tell the actors what to do in a movie or play: *The movie was directed by Joel Coen.*
2 *formal* to tell someone the way to a place: *He directed me to the airport.*
3 to aim something at a particular place, person, etc.: *A lot of advertising is directed at children.*

direction /dəˈrekʃən/ *noun*
the way that someone or something is moving or pointing: *I think we're going in the wrong direction—we should be heading north.* | *He walked in the direction of the house* (= toward the house).

directions /dəˈrekʃənz/ *plural noun*
information about how to get to a place or about how to do something: *Could you give me directions to the airport?* | *Follow the directions on the bottle* (= do what they tell you to do).

directly /dəˈrektli/ *adverb*
1 with no other person, thing, or event involved: *He was driving the car that hit the boys; he is directly responsible for the accident.*
2 exactly in a particular position or direction: *Lucas sat directly behind us.*

director /dəˈrektɚ/ *noun*
1 the person who tells the actors what to do in a movie or play
2 someone who controls an organization or one of its activities: *The director of the museum is in charge of all the employees.*

A. *Find each underlined word on the dictionary page. Write the part of speech and the meaning of the word in the sentence.*

1. The student is showing real <u>progress</u> in his work.

   Part of speech: _____

   Meaning: _____

   _____

2. Because of the bad weather, we didn't make much <u>progress</u> on our trip.

   Part of speech: _____

   Meaning: _____

   _____

3. The concert <u>program</u> didn't give any information about the pianist.

   Part of speech: _____

   Meaning: _____

   _____

4. George <u>programmed</u> his computer to show pictures of his family.

   Part of speech: _____

   Meaning: _____

   _____

(continued)

program[1] /ˈproʊɡræm/ *noun*
1 a show on television or radio: *What's your favorite TV program?* | *We watched a program about whales.*
2 a set of instructions for a computer that makes it do something: *The students are learning how to write computer programs.*
3 a set of organized activities that people do in order to achieve something: *Members of the team have to follow an exercise program.* | *the U.S. space program*
4 a piece of paper or short book that you get at a play, event, or concert that has information about the event and the performers: *The program gave the name of all the performers.*

program[2] *verb* **programmed, programming**
to give a set of instructions to a computer to make it do something: *You can program a computer to play chess.*
–programming *noun* the act or job of writing instructions for a computer: *He's studying computer programming.*

programmer /ˈproʊˌɡræmɚ/ *noun*
someone whose job is writing programs for computers: *a computer programmer*

progress[1] /ˈprɑɡrəs/ *noun*
1 the process of getting better at doing something: *Bob has made good progress in math this year.*
2 the process of getting closer to achieving something: *There has been progress toward peace in the area.*
3 movement toward a place: *The traffic was bad, so we made slow progress.*
4 in progress = happening now: *Please be quiet — there is a test in progress.*

progress[2] /pəˈɡrəs/ *verb, formal*
1 to continue to get better and develop: *Technology is progressing all the time.*
2 to happen or move forward slowly: *I got more and more bored as the meeting progressed.*

5. The business school <u>program</u>
   includes language courses.
   Part of speech: _____
   Meaning: _____

   _____

6. At lunch time, we often listen to a
   news <u>program</u> on the radio.
   Part of speech: _____
   Meaning: _____

   _____

B. *Talk about your answers with another student. Are they the same?*

How Words Are Used

You can learn about how words are used from the example sentences in dictionaries.
These sentences tell you what words often go together.

EXAMPLE

Look at the dictionary page in Exercise 6 on page 67. Read the example sentences.
Then answer these questions.

1. Write the nouns that are used with the adjective *direct*.

   a. direct _____ route _____
   b. direct _____ result _____

2. Write the prepositions that are used with the verb *direct*.

   a. directed _____ by _____
   b. directed _____ to _____
   c. directed _____ at _____

A. *Look at the dictionary page in Exercise 7 on page 68. Use the example sentences to help you find the information.*

1. Write the nouns that are used with the noun *program*.

   a. _____ program

   b. _____ program

   c. _____ program

   d. _____ program

2. Write the verbs that are used with the noun *program*.

   a. _____ program

   b. _____ programs

3. Write the adjectives that are used before the noun *progress*.

   a. _____ progress

   b. _____ progress

4. Write the nouns that are used with the verb *progress*.

   a. _____ is progressing

   b. _____ progressed

B. *Talk about your answers with another student. Are they the same?*

Study Vocabulary Often

To remember words well, you need to see and think about them many times. A vocabulary notebook and word study cards can help you remember new words and build vocabulary.

Vocabulary Notebooks

Get a small notebook and use it only for vocabulary. Write new words in it every day or every week.

How to Write Words in Your Notebook

1. Write the word on the left page. Beside the word, write the part of speech.
2. Below the word, write the sentence or sentences where you found it.
3. Write the dictionary meaning of the word on the right page.
4. Check the pronunciation. Then say the words and meanings aloud. This will help you remember them.

EXAMPLE

1. shell (n)	a hard part on the
It has a very hard	outside of an
shell on its back.	animal, fish, egg,
	or nut

How to Test Yourself with Your Notebook

1. Put your hand over the <u>meanings</u>. Read the words.
2. Can you remember the meanings? Say them aloud if you can.
3. Review the meanings you don't remember.
4. Put your hand over the <u>words</u>. Read the meanings. Can you remember the words?
5. Write the words on a piece of paper. Can you spell them correctly? Then say them aloud.
6. Review the words you don't remember.
7. Go through all the words again the same way. Test yourself often— at least every week.

How to Review Your Notebook with Another Student

1. Give the other student your notebook. Tell him/her to ask you about words or meanings.
2. Write the answers and show them to the other student. Did you spell them correctly?
3. Say the answers aloud if they are correct. Review the words you didn't spell correctly.

A. Look at a story or fable you read in Part 1. Find five new words you want to learn. Write the words in your notebook. Follow the example on page 71.

B. Study your notebook and test yourself.

C. Give your notebook to another student. Ask him or her to test you.

Study Cards

Make study cards for difficult words in your vocabulary notebook. You will need small cards (3 x 5 inches/7 x 12 centimeters).

How to Write Words on the Cards

1. On one side of the card, write the word.
2. Beside the word, write the part of speech.
3. Below the word, write the sentence(s) where you found it.
4. On the other side of the card, write the meaning of the word as it is used in the sentence.
5. Keep the cards with you in a bag or in a pocket. When you have some free time, test yourself. You can do this on the bus or while you are waiting for class.

EXAMPLE

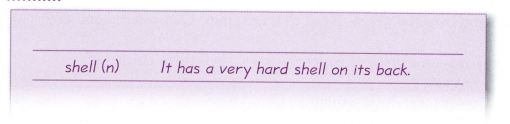

shell (n)   It has a very hard shell on its back.

Front of card

a hard part on the outside of an animal, fish, egg, or nut

Back of card

Using Your Study Cards for Review

How to Test Yourself with Your Cards

1. Look at a word. Can you remember the meaning?
2. Say the word to yourself. If you don't remember it, look at the meaning on the other side.
3. Go through all the cards like this. Review the meanings you didn't remember.
4. Turn the cards over and look at the meanings. Can you remember the words?
5. Say the words to yourself. Then spell them to yourself. Check the words and spelling on the other side.
6. Go through all the cards again like this. Review the words you didn't remember.

How to Review Your Cards with Another Student

1. Give the other student some of your cards. Tell him/her to ask you about words or meanings.
2. Write the answers and show them to the other student. Did you spell them correctly?
3. Say the answers aloud if they are correct. Review the words you didn't spell correctly.

Change Your Cards Often

1. Take out the words you know very well. (You know them well when you can say them very quickly.)
2. Add new words that you want to learn.

EXERCISE 10

A. **On five study cards, write five words you need to learn from your notebook. (You can use the same or different words as in Exercise 11.) Follow the steps above.**

B. **Test yourself with your cards.**

C. **Give your cards to another student. Ask him or her to test you.**

Learning New Words from Your Reading

You will meet many new words when you are reading. You can learn them if you follow some simple steps.

Follow these steps to learn new words when you read:

1. **Read the passage to the end.**
   - Don't stop for new words.

2. **Read the passage again.**
   - Underline the new words and write them down (below the exercise or on a separate piece of paper).

3. **Look up the words in the dictionary.**
   - For each word, write the part of speech and the sentence where you found it.
   - Write the meaning of the word in that sentence.

4. **Write the words in your vocabulary notebook.**
   - Write the parts of speech, the sentences, and the meanings.
   - Check the pronunciation and say the words and meanings aloud.

EXAMPLE

A.   Read the passage to the end. Don't stop for new words.

The turtle is an unusual animal. It has a very hard <u>shell</u> on its back. It has another hard shell under its body. There are many different kinds of turtles. Some of them live in the water. Other turtles live on dry land. They eat mostly plants, but some turtles also eat meat or fish. They don't eat very much. A meal three times a week is enough for them.

B.   Read the passage again. Underline the new words. Write one of them below.

C. Look up the word in the dictionary. Write the part of speech and the sentence where you found it. Then write the meaning of the word in that sentence.

Word: _____ *shell* _____   Part of speech: _____ *noun* _____

Sentence: _*It has a very hard shell on its back.*_____

Meaning: _*a hard part on the outside of an animal, fish, egg, or nut*_____

D. Write the word in your vocabulary notebook. Then check the pronunciation and say the word and meaning aloud.

Remember

When you write a word in your vocabulary notebook, you should also write:
- the part of speech.
- the sentence where you found it.
- the meaning of the word in that sentence.

EXERCISE 1

A. Read the passage to the end.

Sea Turtles—Part 1

Sea turtles are one of the oldest kinds of animals. They are over 100 million years old. That means there were turtles at the time of the dinosaurs. The dinosaurs all died, but the turtles
5 survived.

There are seven kinds of sea turtles in the ocean today. They are generally larger than land turtles. Some sea turtles are huge. They weigh up to 400 pounds (180 kilograms). Sea turtles
10 are different from land turtles in other ways, too. Land turtles have wide shells, and they have space between the top and bottom shells. They can pull in their heads and feet. Sea turtles can't pull in their heads or feet. Their shells are long and
15 narrow. Their front feet, or flippers, are wide and flat. This helps them swim better. In fact, they are very fast in the water. Large sea turtles can swim up to 5.8 mph (9 kph).

(continued)

Sea turtles live in the deep ocean most of the year. For this reason, scientists do not know much about their behavior. But they know that sea turtles move around a lot to find food. Sea turtles can travel hundreds or thousands of miles every year. Some kinds of sea turtles eat only plants. Others eat plants, shellfish, or other sea animals.

20

B. *Read the passage again. Underline the new words. Write five of them below.*

C. *Look up each word in the dictionary. Write the part of speech, the sentence where you found it, and the meaning. Check your work with your teacher. Then write the meaning of the word in that sentence.*

1. Word: _____ Part of speech: _____
   Sentence: _____
   Meaning: _____

2. Word: _____ Part of speech: _____
   Sentence: _____
   Meaning: _____

3. Word: _____ Part of speech: _____
   Sentence: _____
   Meaning: _____

4. Word: _____ Part of speech: _____
   Sentence: _____
   Meaning: _____

5. Word: _____ Part of speech: _____
   Sentence: _____
   Meaning: _____

D. *Write the words in your vocabulary notebook. Then check the pronunciation and say the words and meanings aloud.*

A. Read the passage to the end.

Sea Turtles—Part 2

Can you imagine a hundred baby turtles running on a beach? This is what happens on certain beaches in the Caribbean, the South Pacific, and Southeast Asia.

In fact, once a year, the female sea turtle leaves the ocean. She climbs up onto a beach. She can't walk like a land turtle. She pushes herself through the sand. When she is on dry sand, she lays her eggs—around 100 to 150 of them. Then she pushes herself back down to the water. The eggs remain in the warm sand for about two months.

When the baby sea turtles are born, they have to run for their lives. Birds and other animals are waiting to catch them. The little turtles run down directly toward the ocean. They dive into the water, and they swim fast. In deep water, they will be safer.

Many turtles do not survive this race to safety. Many others die in their first year. That is why female turtles lay lots of eggs. A few turtles always survive. Adult sea turtles have few natural enemies. Only large sharks try to eat them. Sea turtles can live for a very long time—up to 80 years.

B. Read the passage again. Underline the new words. Write five of them below.

C. Look up each word in the dictionary. Write the part of speech, the sentence where you found it, and the meaning. Check your work with your teacher. Then write the meaning of the word in that sentence.

1. Word: _____   Part of speech: _____
   Sentence: _____
   Meaning: _____

2. Word: _____   Part of speech: _____
   Sentence: _____
   Meaning: _____

3. Word: _____   Part of speech: _____
   Sentence: _____
   Meaning: _____

4. Word: _____   Part of speech: _____

Sentence: _____

Meaning: _____

5. Word: _____   Part of speech: _____

Sentence: _____

Meaning: _____

D. *Write the words and the information in your vocabulary notebook. Then check the pronunciation and say the words and meanings aloud.*

EXERCISE 3

A. *Read the passage to the end.*

Sea Turtles—Part 3

Until recently, there were millions of sea turtles in the ocean. They lived in all the warmer parts of the world. They have very few natural enemies, but now they have a new, very serious enemy—humans. Sea turtles are disappearing from the ocean for many reasons. All of these reasons are connected to
5   humans.

First, people kill sea turtles for their meat and their shells. In some countries, there are laws against this. But in the middle of the ocean, laws do not matter very much.

Thousands of turtles are also killed indirectly by humans. They die when
10 they get caught in fishing nets. Or they die in accidents with boats. The pollution of the ocean is another problem. Turtles get sick and die because of dirty water. They can also die when they eat pieces of plastic.

Finally, humans are changing the places where turtles lay their eggs. Around the world, people are building houses, hotels, and roads near beaches.
15 When female turtles come onto the beaches, they may be frightened by noise or lights. They may not lay their eggs. If they lay their eggs, there may be other problems. The eggs may be destroyed by people, cars, or dogs. If baby turtles come out, they may be confused by lights. Instead of running toward the water, they may run away from it.

20 For all these reasons, there are fewer and fewer sea turtles. They survived the dinosaurs, but they may not survive humans.

B. *Read the passage again. Underline the new words. Write five of them below.*

C. *Look up each word in the dictionary. Write the part of speech, the sentence where you found it, and the meaning. Check your work with your teacher. Then write the meaning of the word in that sentence.*

1. Word: _____ Part of speech: _____

   Sentence: _____

   Meaning: _____

2. Word: _____ Part of speech: _____

   Sentence: _____

   Meaning: _____

3. Word: _____ Part of speech: _____

   Sentence: _____

   Meaning: _____

4. Word: _____ Part of speech: _____

   Sentence: _____

   Meaning: _____

5. Word: _____ Part of speech: _____

   Sentence: _____

   Meaning: _____

D. *Write the words in your vocabulary notebook. Then check the pronunciation and say the words and meanings aloud.*

E. *Choose five new words from your notebook that you want to learn. Write them on study cards. (See Part 2, Unit 1, page 72.) Study them alone and then with a partner.*

Remember

When you read, follow the steps for learning new words.
Use your vocabulary notebook and study cards to help you learn them.

The 100 Words

What Are "The 100 Words"?

These words are the most common in written English. About half of the words in any reading are in this list.

Good readers know these words very well. They don't have to look at them for long. They don't have to think about them. Their eyes can move on very quickly. This way, they can read faster and think more about the ideas.

You may know many of the words on this list already. In this unit, you will work with them and get to know them better.

The 100 Words*

a	come	him	new	some	us
about	could	his	no	take	use
after	day	how	not	than	want
all	did	I	now	that	was
also	do	if	of	the	way
an	even	in	on	their	we
and	first	into	one	them	well
any	for	is	only	then	went
are	from	it	or	there	were
as	get	its	other	these	what
at	give	just	our	they	when
back	go	know	out	think	which
be	good	like	over	this	who
because	got	look	people	thought	will
been	had	made	said	time	with
but	has	make	say	to	work
by	have	me	see	took	would
came	he	most	she	two	year
can	her	my	so	up	you
					your

*The Oxford English Corpus lists only the base forms of verbs (*be, have, do, go,* etc.). The list above also includes some other common forms of irregular verbs (*is, are, was, were,* etc.), so there are more than 100 words on this list.

EXERCISE 1

A. *Write in the missing letters. Then write the word.*

1. s <u>a</u> y _____
2. b _ t _____
3. k _ o _ _____
4. w _ s _____
5. b a _ _ _____
6. m _ d _ _____
7. f _ _ _____
8. a _ y _____
9. w i _ l _____
10. w o _ _ d _____
11. o _ t _____
12. s _ m _ _____
13. t i _ _ _____
14. w _ y _____
15. t h _ r_ _____
16. u s _ _____
17. g _ v _ _____
18. j _ s _ _____
19. n e _ _____
20. w e _ t _____
21. y _ _ _____
22. a l _ _ _____
23. l _ k_ _____
24. d a _ _____

B. **Complete the conversation with words from The 100 Words list. The first letter of each word is given.**

Alan: Are you ready f _or_____ coffee?
            ₁

Lynn: Yes, please.

Alan: W_____ y_____ like s _____ milk?
            ₂   ₃   ₄

Lynn: No, thanks. I l _____ my coffee black.
                                      ₅

Alan: M _____ too. H _____ much sugar?
              ₆   ₇

Lynn: J _____ a little, please. I don't like i _____
              ₈   ₉
            too sweet.

C. *Check your answers with your teacher.*

A. *Find the words from the box in the puzzle and circle them. (You can read across or down.)*

after	any	by	for	in	no	some	up
all	are	can	from	most	of	then	way
also	be	did	had	my	or	they	you
and	but	even	he	new	our	to	your

```
N   A   F   T   E   R   F   R   O   M
E   L   Z   O   H   A   D   B   U   T
W   S   R   N   I   N   A   L   L   H
D   O   W   N   W   A   Y   A   R   E
I   M   O   S   T   N   O   C   A   N
D   E   V   E   N   D   U   O   F   A
B   E   F   O   R   E   R   X   T   N
L   Z   O   U   R   S   T   H   E   Y
W   L   R   P   H   A   I   M   O   O
A   N   E   R   E   L   N   E   B   Y
Y   T   O   M   Y   S   O   O   R   C
```

B. *Show your work to another student. Did you find the same words? Then check your answers with your teacher.*

A. *Write in the missing letters. Then write the word.*

1. o _ l _ _____
2. a b _ _ t _____
3. t h _ s _ _____
4. w _ _ k _____
5. t h _ _ r _____
6. w h i _ _ _____
7. y o _ _ _____
8. p e _ p _ _ _____

9. t h _ y _____
10. w e _ e _____
11. s _ _ d _____
12. f r _ _ _____
13. t h _ _ k _____
14. c _ _ l d _____
15. a f _ _ _ _____
16. t _ _ k _____

17. t _ k _   _____
18. n _ t   _____
19. i _ _ o   _____
20. w _ _ n   _____

21. w a _ _   _____
22. t h o _ g _ _ _____
23. a _ d   _____
24. t _ _ t   _____

B. Complete the conversation with words from The 100 Words list. The first letter of each word is given.

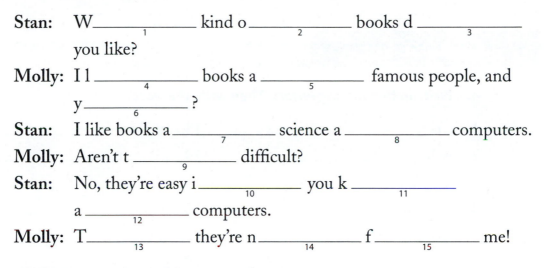

Stan: W_____ kind o_____ books d_____
              1   2   3
      you like?

Molly: I l_____ books a_____ famous people, and
            4   5
      y_____?
        6

Stan: I like books a_____ science a_____ computers.
                   7   8

Molly: Aren't t_____ difficult?
            9

Stan: No, they're easy i_____ you k_____
                      10   11
      a_____ computers.
        12

Molly: T_____ they're n_____ f_____ me!
        13   14   15

C. Check your answers with your teacher.

EXERCISE 4

A. Find 20 words from The 100 Words list and circle them. (You can read across or down.) Then write the words below.

```
B  E  C  A  U  S  E  L  N  O
U  P  O  N  L  Y  N  H  E  R
T  H  U  D  S  H  E  T  W  O
T  A  L  R  O  N  W  H  O  W
H  F  R  O  M  A  E  A  U  I
I  T  T  H  E  S  E  N  L  L
S  E  E  A  Y  G  O  O  D  L
O  R  I  V  E  T  H  I  N  K
M  A  K  E  A  O  A  T  T  O
A  L  S  O  R  W  T  A  K  E
```

_____ _____ _____ _____

_____ _____ _____ _____

_____ _____ _____ _____

_____ _____ _____ _____

B. *Show your work to another student. Did you find the same words? Then check your answers with your teacher.*

EXERCISE 5

A. *Write in the missing letters. Then write the word.*

1. c o _ _ _____
2. w h _ _____
3. m _ k _ _____
4. b _ _ n _____
5. w _ a _ _____
6. h _ v _ _____
7. t _ m _ _____
8. t _ i _ _____
9. h _ w _____
10. g o _ _____
11. o v _ _ _____
12. t _ _ m _____

13. m _ s _ _____
14. f i _ _ t _____
15. c a _ _ _____
16. w _ t _ _____
17. w o _ _ d _____
18. e _ _ n _____
19. y e _ _ _____
20. o t h _ _ _____
21. l _ _ k _____
22. g _ _ d _____
23. b e c _ _ _ _ _____
24. o _ r _____

B. *Complete the conversation with words from The 100 Words list. The first letter of each word is given.*

Randy: Excuse m_____₁! Is t_____₂ yours?

Silvia: Oh, yes. Thanks. Where d_____₃ y_____₄ find i_____₅?

Randy: Right here o_____₆ t_____₇ ground. It fell o_____₈ of y_____₉ bag.

Silvia: W_____₁₀, thanks again.

Randy: M_____₁₁ name's Randy. W_____₁₂'s yours?

Silvia: Silvia.

Randy: A _____ y_____ a student here?

13   14

Silvia: No, I w_____ at t_____ gym. I teach yoga.

15   16

Randy: Oh! I g_____ t_____ the gym o_____

17   18   19

Fridays. I'll l _____ for you next t_____ I'm

20   21

t_____.

22

C. *Check your answers with your teacher.*

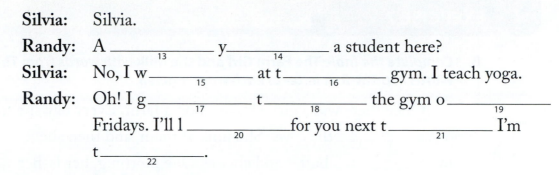

EXERCISE 6

A. *Find 20 words from The 100 Words list and circle them. (You can read across or down.) Then write the words below.*

```
I   T   S   M   Y   F   I   R   S   T
F   K   W   E   L   L   N   W   A   Y
I   N   T   H   O   U   G   H   T   O
T   O   P   I   G   O   O   A   S   V
S   W   E   N   T   T   T   S   T   E
T   O   O   K   W   H   I   C   H   V
O   R   P   W   H   E   N   O   E   E
M   K   L   W   I   R   E   U   I   N
B   E   E   N   C   E   L   L   R   B
A   L   S   O   H   M   A   D   E   D
```

_____   _____   _____   _____

_____   _____   _____   _____

_____   _____   _____   _____

_____   _____   _____   _____

_____   _____   _____   _____

B. *Show your work to another student. Did you find the same words? Then check your answers with your teacher.*

A. *Complete the fable* **The Farm Girl and the Milk** *with words from The 100 Words list. The first letter of each word is given.*

Once there was a girl who lived on a farm. Every day she took care o_____ (1) the cows. She milked them, and then she m_____ (2) butter and cheese. One morning, her father s_____ (3), "You are a g_____ (4) girl. You w_____ (5) very hard. You can have s_____ (6) of the milk this morning. You can t_____ (7) it to town and sell it at the market. Then you c_____ (8) keep the money and buy something nice."

The farm girl started on the road to town w_____ (9) the milk. On the way, she thought. "This is g_____ (10) milk. I can sell it f_____ (11) a price. Then I can buy s_____ (12) eggs. I'll bring those eggs home and keep t_____ (13). Soon I'll have chickens. Chickens grow fast. In a few months, I'll have m_____ (14) eggs and chickens. T_____ (15) I can sell the chickens and keep the money. I_____ (16) a few more months, I'll h_____ (17) enough money for a n_____ (18) dress."

The farm girl c_____ (19) see the town now. It was n_____ (20) far away. "I'll buy a beautiful dress," she t_____ (21). "It'll be blue and gold. It'll be the m_____ (22) beautiful dress in town. All the young men will l_____ (23) at me. But I won't talk to any of them. I'll wait f_____ (24) a rich man or a prince. Yes, a prince. He'll see m_____ (25) and fall in love. I'll marry a prince."

The farm girl w_____ (26) very happy. She closed her eyes, thinking a_____ (27) the prince. She didn't s_____ (28) a large stone in the road. H_____ (29) foot hit the stone and down she went. Down w_____ (30) the milk, too, all over the road. And that was the end of the eggs, the chickens, the dress, and the prince.

B. *Look at the passage again. Find more words from The 100 Words list and circle them. Then check your answers on page 80.*

Guessing Meaning from Context

What Is Context?

Context is the sentence or sentences around a word. From the context, you can learn a lot about a word.

- You can learn the part of speech.
- You can often understand the general meaning.

EXAMPLE

Read the sentences. Write the part of speech of the missing word (noun, verb, adjective, or adverb). Then find the missing word in the box and write it in the sentence.

Mara Milvaney is 36 years old. Mara and her family live in a small _____*town*_____ in Australia.

tree	horse	quiet	town	begin	when

Part of speech: _____*noun*_____

Explanation:

- Only a noun can follow the words *in a small*.
- The nouns in the box are *tree*, *horse*, and *town*.
- The word means something people *live in*. People don't live in a horse or a tree. *Town* is the best answer.

Note: Groups of words (phrases) often work together like one word. (See Part 2, Unit 6, page 106.) In these exercises, you will find some phrases. You should learn and read them the same way you learn and read single words.

Examples: Sergio often <u>listens to</u> music.
<u>How far</u> is the station?

A. *Read each sentence. Find the missing word in the box and write it in the sentence. Then write the part of speech of the missing word.*

1. Mara Milvaney is 36 years old. Mara and her family live in a small town in Australia. Mara and her husband, Dan, have three children, two boys and a _____.

house	young	love	girl	sheep	live

   Part of speech: _____

2. They live in a small house with a large yard. The children _____ animals very much. The family has three cats, two dogs, and a horse.

meat	like	have	free	buy	full

   Part of speech: _____

3. Mara and Dan have a sheep farm. They sell some of the young sheep for meat. People in Europe and the United States buy the meat. It's expensive but very _____.

easy	early	good	cheap	work	baby

   Part of speech: _____

4. Mara and her family have to work _____. The children often help their parents. There's always something to do on a farm.

before	away	business	earth	hard	feel

   Part of speech: _____

B. *Talk about your answers with another student. Are they the same?*

A. *Read each sentence. Find the missing word in the box and write it in the sentence. Then write the part of speech of the missing word.*

1. Malcolm Morris is 29 years old. He lives in Charlotteville, Tobago. Tobago is a small island country in the Caribbean Sea. Malcolm's town is near the _____.

swim	evening	sea	warm	sun	beautiful

   Part of speech: _____

2. Malcolm is a fisherman. He has a small blue and red boat. Malcolm and the other fishermen _____ their boats on the beach.

drive	large	sand	water	find	keep

   Part of speech: _____

3. Early every morning, Malcolm takes his boat out fishing. When he has _____ fish, he comes back to the town.

far	land	free	food	eat	enough

   Part of speech: _____

4. In the afternoon, he sleeps for a while. Then he works on his boat, or he sits in a café with his _____. They like to talk about fishing and life.

fish	teachers	often	friends	new	drink

   Part of speech: _____

B. *Talk about your answers with another student. Are they the same?*

A. *Read the passage to the end. Think about the part of speech of each missing word. Then complete the passage with words from the box.*

help	place	milk	find	north	summer

John Utsi lives in Jokkmokk, a small city in Sweden. He's 43 years old, and he's a writer for a newspaper. John and his family are Sami people. In the past, the Sami people lived in the _____ 1 of Sweden. They kept reindeer. The reindeer had to move often to _____ 2 food. The Sami people didn't have homes in one _____ 3. They moved with the reindeer, and they lived in tents. From the reindeer, they got _____ 4, meat, and warm clothes.

John, his wife, Elin, and their two daughters live in the city most of the year. John works for a newspaper. But every _____ 5, the family goes to Lake Kutjaure. They live in a tent like Sami people did in the past. John and Elin _____ 6 John's brother. He has lots of reindeer.

B. *Talk about your answers with another student. Are they the same?*

A. Read the passage to the end. Think about the part of speech of each missing word. Then think of words to complete the passage. (More than one word is possible for each blank.)

Leimomi Mapuana lives on the island of Hawaii. She's 9 years old. Her _____ is native Hawaiian. The native Hawaiians lived in Hawaii before Americans or Europeans _____ to the island.

Leimomi's parents have a farm. They grow fruit and _____. Her father also has a boat, and he goes fishing.

Leimomi goes to elementary school. In some ways, her school is like other elementary schools in the United States. The children _____ reading, writing, math, science, history, and geography. But in other ways, it's very _____. In this school, the children speak English only in their English lesson. For their other lessons, they _____ Hawaiian. And they learn about their Hawaiian history and Hawaiian music, stories, and dancing.

B. Talk about your answers with another student. Are they the same? Then check your answers with your teacher.

A. *Read the passage to the end. Think about the part of speech of the missing words. Then think of words to complete the passage. (More than one word is possible for each blank.)*

Valeriy Korotkov is 45 years old. He lives in the town of Yeniseysk in Russia, but he doesn't work in Yeniseysk. He _____ all over Russia. Valeriy's job isn't like most jobs. He's a firefighter, but he doesn't fight fires in _____ or other buildings. He fights forest fires.

He works with a _____ of other firefighters. When there's a forest fire, they get on a plane. The plane _____ near the fire, and the firefighters jump out of the plane. They land on the ground, and then they work _____ to stop the fire. This isn't always easy when it's a _____ fire. When lots of trees are burning, it can be dangerous. Sometimes firefighters are _____. Once Valeriy broke his leg. Another time he burned his hand.

But Valeriy likes his job very much. He likes jumping from the planes, and he likes working outside. "I could _____ work in an office!" he says.

B. *Talk about your answers with another student. Are they the same? Then check your answers with your teacher.*

Guessing Word Meanings

The context around a word can help you guess the meaning. You may only understand the general meaning. But that may be enough to follow the ideas or the story. You don't always need to know the dictionary meaning.

How Can the Context Help You Guess Meaning?

In the context, you may find
. . . information about the word.
. . . a word that means the same thing.
. . . a word that means the opposite (for example: *long/short, new/old*).

EXAMPLE

> *Read the context around each underlined word or phrase. Then write the part of speech and the general meaning. Don't use a dictionary.*

1. Can you see that <u>nest</u> in the tree? There are four baby birds in it. They're calling for their mother. Look! Now the mother bird is coming. She has some food for the babies.

   Part of speech: _____ *noun* _____
   General meaning: _*a place where birds live and keep their babies*_

   Explanation:
   • It's something in a tree.
   • It has baby birds in it.
   • The mother bird also lives in it.

2. Ben's mother brought him close to the horse. He didn't want to touch it because he was afraid. "You can touch it on the nose," she said. "<u>Go ahead</u>. It's okay. It won't do anything. It's a very nice horse."

   Part of speech: _*phrasal verb (verb + preposition)*_
   General meaning: _*You can do it.*_

   Explanation:
   • It's something a mother says to a child.
   • You can say it when someone is afraid or not sure about something.
   • You say it to help them do something.

3. Please leave those bananas. They aren't <u>ripe</u>. They're still very green. We can't eat them today. We'll eat them in a few days.

Part of speech: _____*adjective*_____

General meaning: _____*ready to eat*_____

Explanation:
- It's used to talk about fruit.
- It tells about when you can eat fruit.
- It means the opposite of *green*.

Note: You should NOT use a dictionary in these exercises until after you guess the general meaning.

EXERCISE 6

A. Read the context around each underlined word or phrase. Then write the part of speech and the general meaning. Don't use a dictionary.

1. My friend Raymond is a very <u>lazy</u> person. He doesn't like to work. He doesn't like to play sports. He likes to sit and watch television. And he likes to sleep.

   Part of speech: _____

   General meaning: _____

2. My wife and I want to buy a new car, but we don't have much money. We can't ask my father for help. We have to go to the bank. I hope they will give us a <u>loan</u>.

   Part of speech: _____

   General meaning: _____

3. Roger often has <u>nightmares</u>. In the middle of the night, he wakes up and calls for me. I go talk to him and stay with him. He doesn't want to go back to sleep because he's afraid.

   Part of speech: _____

   General meaning: _____

4. The cat has to go to the vet (animal doctor). First, we'll put her in a <u>cage</u>. Then we'll put the <u>cage</u> in the car. That way she can't run around the car. An angry cat is dangerous in a car.

Part of speech: _____

General meaning: _____

5. Owen ran fast to <u>catch up with</u> his friends. But his friends ran fast, too. They turned a corner, and then he couldn't see them anymore.

Part of speech: _____

General meaning: _____

B. *Talk about your answers with another student. Are they the same?*

C. *Look up the words in a dictionary. Correct your answers if necessary. Then check your answers with your teacher.*

EXERCISE 7

A. *Read the context around each underlined word or phrase. Then write the part of speech and the general meaning. Don't use a dictionary.*

1. Marek was a <u>brilliant</u> student. He got the highest marks in all his classes, and he finished college early. Now he has a very good job.

Part of speech: _____

General meaning: _____

2. The country around here is beautiful in March and April. That's the time when the fruit trees <u>bloom</u>. Some trees have pink flowers, and some have white flowers.

Part of speech: _____

General meaning: _____

3. The restaurant last night was <u>awful</u>. We had to wait for a long time. The meat was cold, the vegetables were cooked too much, and the coffee was terrible.

    Part of speech: _____

    General meaning: _____

4. The letter was very <u>brief</u>. It gave only the date and the time of the meeting. It didn't tell me what the meeting was about.

    Part of speech: _____

    General meaning: _____

5. There were toys <u>all over</u> the floor. But the children were happy. They sat in the middle of all the toys and played.

    Part of speech: _____

    General meaning: _____

B. *Talk about your answers with another student. Are they the same?*

C. *Look up the words in a dictionary. Correct your answers if necessary. Then check your answers with your teacher.*

EXERCISE 8

A. *Read the context around each underlined word or phrase. Then write the part of speech and the general meaning. Don't use a dictionary.*

1. Some people <u>complain</u> a lot. They're never happy with things. They always see the bad side, and they tell everyone about it. These people are not fun to be with.

    Part of speech: _____

    General meaning: _____

2. I like your <u>outfit</u>. That shirt is very nice with those pants. Where did you buy them? I need to find something like that for the party next week.

    Part of speech: _____

    General meaning: _____

3. After tennis yesterday, my feet were <u>sore</u>. I think I need to get different shoes. These shoes hurt my feet every time I wear them.

Part of speech: _____

General meaning: _____

4. First, Dennis heard the bad news from Samia. She always knew everything about the company. Then he got the <u>official</u> letter. It said he had to leave his job at the end of the month.

Part of speech: _____

General meaning: _____

5. Shana worked in Atlanta, Pittsburgh, and Seattle. Then she got a job in Portland. She liked the city, so she decided to <u>settle</u> there. Now she's married and has two children.

Part of speech: _____

General meaning: _____

B. Talk about your answers with another student. Are they the same?

C. Look up the words in a dictionary. Correct your answers if necessary. Then check your answers with your teacher.

A. *Read the context around each underlined word or phrase. Then write the part of speech and the general meaning. Don't use a dictionary.*

1. Can you please help me? I can't take this dress off. There's a <u>hook</u> in the back. I can't reach it. Can you do it?

   Part of speech: _____

   General meaning: _____

2. In Scotland you often see <u>herds</u> of sheep. Sometimes they're walking in the middle of the road. You have to stop and wait for them to get out of the way.

   Part of speech: _____

   General meaning: _____

3. Pavel is looking for a job after school. He called to <u>inquire</u> about one at the supermarket. But they said they don't need people now.

   Part of speech: _____

   General meaning: _____

4. This water bottle has a <u>leak</u>. I put it in my bag yesterday. When I opened my bag later, it was all wet inside. My books and papers got wet, too.

   Part of speech: _____

   General meaning: _____

5. Please <u>fold</u> a piece of paper in half. Then open it again. Now you have two sides with a line in the middle. Write the words on the left and the meanings on the right.

   Part of speech: _____

   General meaning: _____

B. *Talk about your answers with another student. Are they the same?*

C. *Look up the words in a dictionary. Correct your answers if necessary. Then check your answers with your teacher.*

A. *Read the context around each underlined word or phrase. Then write the part of speech and the general meaning. Don't use a dictionary.*

1. There was a fire on my street. The people next door called the firefighters. They came and <u>put out</u> the fire. The house was still standing, but it was all burned inside.

   Part of speech: _____

   General meaning: _____

2. My sister is very <u>fond of</u> her cat. She buys toys for it, and she gives it fresh meat and fish. She doesn't give it cat food.

   Part of speech: _____

   General meaning: _____

3. He put the wet clothes outside to dry in the sun. But then it got cloudy. At the end of the day, the clothes were still <u>damp</u>.

   Part of speech: _____

   General meaning: _____

4. Don't wash your new T-shirt in very hot water. It will <u>shrink</u>. Then it will be too small for you. Wash it in cold water.

   Part of speech: _____

   General meaning: _____

5. He was a very <u>greedy</u> little boy. First, he had some ice cream. Then he had a piece of cake. He still wasn't full, so he ate a chocolate bar.

   Part of speech: _____

   General meaning: _____

B. *Talk about your answers with another student. Are they the same?*

C. *Look up the words in a dictionary. Correct your answers if necessary. Then check your answers with your teacher.*

Word Parts

Words are often made of different parts. If you notice the parts, you can understand words better.

The root is the most important part of a word.

>   *Example:*   happy

A prefix is a part added before the root.

>   *Example:*   un + happy = unhappy

A suffix is a part added after a root.

>   *Example:*   happy + ness = happiness

Prefixes

A prefix before a root changes the meaning.

EXAMPLE

unhappy   Prefix: ___*un-*___   Meaning of prefix: _____*not*_____
             Root: ___*happy*___   Meaning of root with prefix: ___*not happy*___

> **Note:** There are many prefixes that mean *not*. Here are some of them: *dis-, im-, non-, un.*

EXERCISE 1

A. ***The words below have two parts: a prefix and a root. Write the prefix and its meaning from the box. Then write the roots. (The meaning not can be used more than once.)***

Prefixes	Meanings
dis- non- un- mis- pre- under-	not under badly before

1. unfriendly   unafraid   unhealthy   unkind   unreal

   Prefix: _____ Meaning of prefix: _____

   Roots: _____

2. underground   underwater   underpass   undershirt   underline

   Prefix: _____ Meaning of prefix: _____

   Roots: _____

3. misspell   misuse   misunderstand   misplace   mislead

   Prefix: _____ Meaning of prefix: _____

   Roots: _____

4. preschool   preposition   prepay   preview   prehistoric

   Prefix: _____ Meaning of prefix: _____

   Roots: _____

5. dislike   disappear   discolor   disbelieve   discontinue

   Prefix: _____ Meaning of prefix: _____

   Roots: _____

6. nonstop   nonsense   nonfiction   nonsmoker   nonviolent

   Prefix: _____ Meaning of prefix: _____

   Roots: _____

B. *Talk about your answers with another student. Are they the same?*

C. *Look up the meaning of any new words and write them in your vocabulary notebook.*

Suffixes

A suffix after the root changes the meaning and often changes the part of speech.

EXAMPLE

happiness   Suffix: ___-ness___   Root: _____happy_____

Part of speech: root alone _adjective_   root with suffix ___noun___

> **Note:** Sometimes the spelling of the root changes when you add a suffix.
>
> **Example:** happy → happiness (y → i)

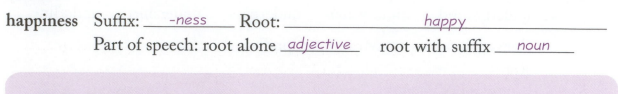

EXERCISE 2

A. *The words below have two parts: a root and a suffix. Write the suffix from the box. Then write the roots and the parts of speech.*

Suffixes					
-er	-est	-ful	-less	-ly	-ness

1. worker   teacher   helper   driver   farmer

   Suffix: _____ Roots: _____

   Parts of speech: root alone _____ root with suffix _____

2. loudly   lightly   deeply   closely   really

   Suffix: _____ Roots: _____

   Parts of speech: root alone _____ root with suffix _____

3. darkness   goodness   hardness   emptiness   sleepiness

   Suffix: _____ Roots: _____

   Parts of speech: root alone _____ root with suffix _____

4. warmer   earlier   later   fatter   higher

   Suffix: _____ Roots: _____

   Parts of speech: root alone _____ root with suffix _____

5. useful   wonderful   thankful   helpful   careful

Suffix: _____ Roots: _____

Parts of speech: root alone _____ root with suffix _____

6. careless   homeless   friendless   helpless   childless

Suffix: _____ Roots: _____

Parts of speech: root alone _____ root with suffix _____

7. biggest   heaviest   dirtiest   loudest   sweetest

Suffix: _____ Roots: _____

Parts of speech: root alone _____ root with suffix _____

B. *Talk about your answers with another student. Are they the same?*

C. *Look up the meaning of any new words and write them in your vocabulary notebook.*

Word Families

A word family is a group of words with the same root. They all belong to the same "family" of meaning, but they are different parts of speech.

The parts of speech are formed differently in each word family. Sometimes you need to

   . . . add a suffix. **Example:** beauty → beautiful
   . . . add a prefix. **Example:** live → alive
   . . . change the root. **Example:** strong → strength

> **Note:** The same word form can sometimes be more than one part of speech.
>
>   **Example:** *anger* (noun and verb)
>
> There may be more than one form for a part of speech.
>
>   **Example:** *alive, lively* (adjectives)
>
> You may not find all the parts of speech in every word family.

EXAMPLE

Noun	Verb	Adjective	Adverb
beauty	*beautify*	*beautiful*	*beautifully*

A. *Work with another student. Write the <u>adjective</u> and <u>adverb</u> forms for each noun. Don't use a dictionary. If you don't know a form, make a guess.*

Nouns	Adjectives	Adverbs
1. stranger	strange	strangely
2. effect	_____	_____
3. sleep	_____	_____
4. fear	_____	_____
5. light	_____	_____
6. help	_____	_____
7. difference	_____	_____
8. color	_____	_____

B. *Check your work in the dictionary. Correct your answers if necessary. Then write any new words in your vocabulary notebook.*

A. *Work with another student. Write the <u>noun</u> and <u>verb</u> forms for each adjective. Don't use a dictionary. If you don't know a form, make a guess.*

Adjectives	Nouns	Verbs
1. sad	_____	_____
2. empty	_____	_____
3. hot	_____	_____
4. open	_____	_____
5. strong	_____	_____
6. dark	_____	_____

B. *Check your work in the dictionary. Correct your answers if necessary. Then write any new words in your vocabulary notebook.*

EXERCISE 5

A. *Work with another student. Write the <u>noun</u> and <u>adverb</u> forms for each adjective. Don't use a dictionary. If you don't know a form, make a guess.*

Adjectives	Nouns	Adverbs
1. warm	_____	_____
2. cold	_____	_____
3. heavy	_____	_____
4. hungry	_____	_____
5. kind	_____	_____
6. angry	_____	_____
7. loud	_____	_____
8. high	_____	_____

B. *Check your work in the dictionary. Correct your answers if necessary. Then write any new words in your vocabulary notebook.*

EXERCISE 6

A. *Work with another student. Write the <u>noun</u>, <u>verb</u>, and <u>adverb</u> forms for each adjective. Don't use a dictionary. If you don't know a form, make a guess.*

Adjectives	Nouns	Verbs	Adverbs
1. clean	_____	_____	_____
2. dangerous	_____	_____	_____
3. free	_____	_____	_____
4. direct	_____	_____	_____
5. weak	_____	_____	_____
6. sweet	_____	_____	_____
7. real	_____	_____	_____
8. deep	_____	_____	_____

B. *Check your work in the dictionary. Correct your answers if necessary. Then write any new words in your vocabulary notebook.*

How Words Are Used Together

Understanding a sentence is not always simple. It means more than understanding each word and then putting the words together.

You need to understand

. . . how words are used in phrases.
. . . how to find the key parts of sentences.
. . . how pronouns work in sentences.

How Words Are Used in Phrases

Some groups of words are often used together. These groups—or phrases—are used in speaking and in writing. You can better understand what you read if you know these phrases.

Some Common Kinds of Phrases

In these exercises, you will work with some common phrases. There are many, many others in English. It's important to learn phrases the same way you learn vocabulary words.

When you are reading, you should notice phrases and look them up in your dictionary. Then write them in your vocabulary notebook and on your study cards.

Verb + noun: Does Marco <u>play tennis</u>?

Phrasal verbs (verb + preposition): He was tired, so he <u>sat down</u>.

Prepositional phrases: There was a park <u>at the end</u> of the street.

Adverbial phrases: The bus is never <u>on time</u>.

Phrases are often different in different languages.
- How do you say *sit down* in your language? Do you use a phrasal verb?
- How do you say *play tennis* in your language? Is the verb for *play tennis* the same as the verb for *play the piano* in your language?

A. *Think about the phrases in these sentences. How do you say them in your language? Write the phrase in your language.*

Phrases in English	Phrases in Your Language
1. I <u>go swimming</u> once a week.	_____
2. What time did you <u>get up</u> this morning?	_____
3. My sister is coming home <u>next week</u>.	_____
4. Did you <u>walk the dog</u>?	_____
5. The gas station is <u>on the right</u>.	_____
6. Hank shouts <u>all the time</u>.	_____
7. He's arriving <u>by train</u>.	_____
8. I <u>had breakfast</u> early this morning.	_____

B. *Talk about the phrases with another student.*

- If you speak the same language, check the other student's phrases. Are they the same as yours?
- If you speak different languages, explain your phrases to the other student. Which ones, if any, are like English?

EXERCISE 2

A. *Underline the phrasal verb(s) from the box in these sentences. Some phrases are used more than once. (Note: The verbs may be in a different form—* get up → gets up.)

fall down	get out	lie down	put on	turn off
get off	get up	look up	take off	wait for

1. Sharon gets up early every morning to take the train.
2. It's late. Please turn off that music. I want to go to sleep.
3. I'm waiting for my son. He gets out of school at 3:00 P.M.
4. Brian got off the bus at the last stop.

5. Stacy fell down and hurt her leg. She couldn't get up.

6. Please come in. You can take off your coat and leave it here.

7. I wasn't feeling very well, and I wanted to lie down.

8. Roy needed to know the name of the Brazilian president. He looked it up on the Internet.

9. Sanford put on his shoes and went outside.

10. Nat was ready to go home, but he had to wait for his brother.

B. *Complete each sentence with a phrasal verb from the box in part A. Use each one only once. (You may change the form of the verb.)*

1. I'll _____ that word in the dictionary.

2. There was a big storm last night. A large tree in our yard _____.

3. I always _____ the lights when I leave a room.

4. After lunch, Susanna often goes to her room. She _____ for an hour and reads.

5. When I _____ this morning, it was still dark.

6. The trip to Boston took four hours. When Vince _____ the train in South Station, he looked for Sally. But she wasn't there.

7. It was very cold that day. Thomas _____ a warm jacket. He also wore his gloves.

8. Paul stayed in the classroom to talk with the teacher. Yvonne _____ him outside.

9. What time do you _____ of work today?

10. _____ your shoes. They're all wet. I'll give you some dry socks.

C. *Talk about your answers with another student. Are they the same?*

A. *Underline the adverbial phrase(s) from the box in each sentence. Some phrases are used more than once.*

after a while	all the time	at last	on time
all day long	at first	for now	right away

1. Rita is finishing high school this year. She's not sure what to do after that. For now she doesn't want to go to college. She wants to get a job.

2. The students didn't like the new professor at first. She didn't smile much. But after a while, they began to like her more. She was really very nice.

3. The train is often late, but this morning it was on time. I got to the office early and started to work right away. I had a lot of work to do.

4. Miriam studies in her room all the time. She doesn't go out often, and she never watches television. She says she wants to get good grades.

5. He waited all day long for her phone call. At last, in the evening, the phone rang. He answered it right away, but it wasn't her.

6. You can leave your bag here for now, but please come get it before noon. This is a busy place.

7. He didn't feel well that morning, so he went home early. But after a while, he felt better, and he went back to work.

8. After ten years, he still looked the same. I knew him right away.

B. *Complete each sentence with an adverbial phrase from the box in part A. Use each one only once.*

1. Sam is living with some friends _____. Next month he'll look for an apartment.

2. Jessica is never _____ for class. She always comes in late.

3. _____, Sean stopped the video. He only wanted to watch the first part.

(continued)

4. _____, she thought he was angry, but then she saw him smile.

5. When Reuben heard the news, he called his mother _____.

6. The men started working early in the morning and worked _____. In the evening, the job was done.

7. My dog is still young, and he wants to play _____.

8. _____ the rain stopped, and we went out for a walk.

C. Talk about your answers with another student. Are they the same?

EXERCISE 4

A. Underline the prepositional phrase from the box in each sentence.

in back of	in the middle of	on the right
in front of	next to	on top of

1. There was a bag of trash in the middle of the road.

2. A new restaurant opened up next to the police station.

3. There was a beautiful garden in back of the house. You couldn't see it from the street.

4. If you walk down the street, the library is on the right.

5. The bus stop is in front of the book shop. You can look at books while you wait for the bus.

6. He left his coffee cup on top of the car.

B. Complete each sentence with a prepositional phrase from the box in part A. (Note: More than one answer is possible in some of the blanks.)

1. The line for tickets was short. There were only two people _____ me.

2. A very big tree grew _____ the garden. There were flowers all around it.

3. The cheese is _____ the refrigerator. I put it there so the dog can't get it.

4. He built a little house _____ the store. He slept and ate his meals there. That way, he was never far from the store.
5. It's easy to find South Street. On the left is the post office. _____ _____, there's a gas station. South Street is in between.
6. Lenya stood _____ her friend Sasha. Lenya was much shorter and she looked much younger.

C. Talk about your answers with another student. Are they the same?

How to Find the Key Parts of Sentences

The key parts of sentences are the subject and the verb.
- The **subject** tells who or what the sentence is about.
- The **verb** tells what the subject does or it gives information about the subject.

EXAMPLE

Underline the subject and verb in each sentence. Write S under the subject and V under the verb.

1. <u>Suki</u> <u>works</u> in a hospital.
   S   V

   Explanation:
   - The sentence is about *Suki*.
   - The verb *works* tells what the subject does.

2. <u>Many towns and cities</u> <u>have</u> traffic problems.
   S   V

   Explanation:
   - The sentence is about *many towns and cities*.
   - Note that the subject can be plural. It can also be more than one word.
   - The verb *have* gives information about the subject.

3. <u>A very large bird</u> <u>is sitting</u> in the tree.
   S   V

   Explanation:
   - The sentence is about *a very large bird*.
   - The verb *is sitting* tells what the subject does.
   - Note that the verb can have more than one part.

A. *Underline the subject and verb in each sentence. Write S under the subject and V under the verb.*

1. Saffa speaks many different languages.
2. She speaks English, French, and Arabic.
3. Her family is from Morocco.
4. But now they live in Denver.
5. Saffa is taking a Spanish course.
6. Many Spanish-speaking people live in Denver.
7. Some of these people speak only Spanish.
8. They sometimes have problems in school and at work.
9. The Spanish course is not hard for Saffa.
10. Soon she'll finish it.
11. Then she'll look for a job.
12. Many companies look for people who speak Spanish and English.

B. *Talk about your answers with another student. Are they the same?*

A. *Underline the subject and verb in each sentence. Write S under the subject and V under the verb.*

1. Movies are big business in India.
2. Every year Indians make almost 1,000 movies.
3. Millions of Indian people watch these movies.
4. They like Indian movies better than American or European movies.
5. Indian movies sometimes have sad parts.
6. But they almost always end happily.
7. Music is also an important part of every movie.
8. Every movie has a beautiful woman and a love story.
9. Asha Sachdev stars in many movies.
10. Indian people all know and love Asha's face.

11. People see her face on the walls.

12. Big pictures of her face are all around Indian cities.

B. *Talk about your answers with another student. Are they the same?*

How Pronouns Work in Sentences

Pronouns are small but important words. They are often important in the meanings of sentences.

Personal Pronouns and Possessive Adjectives

Subject pronouns:	I	you	he	she	it	we	they
Object pronouns:	me	you	him	her	it	us	them
Possessive adjectives:	my	your	his	her	its	our	their

A personal pronoun takes the place of a noun or noun phrase. It can be the *subject* of the sentence.

> *Example:* Ken loves to grow flowers. He has lots of roses.

Or it can be the *object* of a verb or preposition.

> *Example:* Ken loves to grow flowers. He has lots of them. Sometimes he gives them to his friends.

A possessive adjective shows that something belongs to someone (or something).

> *Example:* Sometimes he gives them to his friends.

EXAMPLE
· · · · · · · · · ·

> *Underline the personal pronouns and possessive adjectives in the sentences. Write S under the subject pronouns, O under the object pronouns, and P under the possessive adjectives.*
>
> Ken loves to grow flowers. He has lots of them in his back yard. Sometimes
> <u>S</u>   <u>O</u>   <u>P</u>
> he gives them to his friends.
> <u>S</u>   <u>O</u>   <u>P</u>

A. *Underline the personal pronouns and possessive adjectives in the sentences. Write S under the subject pronouns, O under the object pronouns, and P under the possessive adjectives.*

1. Liz has two little girls. Their names are Anna and Piper. They go to school on the school bus.

2. Dan is a teacher in Los Angeles. He teaches at a night school. His students are men and women from many different countries. They are learning English in Dan's class.

3. Diego is a doctor in a city hospital. Some of his patients are rich people. They pay him well. But some of his patients are poor people. They don't have very much money. Diego takes care of them for free.

4. Rhonda loves going to the movies with her friends. Every Friday night she goes to see a movie with them. Last Friday she saw an Italian movie. She said it was very good.

5. Alex built a new house for his family. He worked on it for two years. Now the house is finished. He and his family moved in last week. They are very happy with it.

6. Bob likes making bread. He makes many kinds of bread. All of his bread is very good, but his French bread is the best. It tastes just like the bread in Paris.

7. Evita has two jobs. Her first job is at a school. She teaches reading and writing to high school students. Her second job is at home. She writes books for young people. Her students sometimes like to read them.

8. Paul moved from Houston, in the United States, to Santiago, in Chile. At first, he didn't know many people. Then he made some new friends. They were very kind to him. They took him to visit many interesting places.

B. *Talk about your answers with another student. Are they the same?*

A. *Complete the passage with personal pronouns or possessive adjectives. Use words from the box.*

Subject pronouns:	I	you	he	she	it	we	they
Object pronouns:	me	you	him	her	it	us	them
Possessive adjectives:	my	your	his	her	its	our	their

Estrella and her sister Ana live in San Diego, California.

_____ came to San Diego just two years ago from El Salvador.
    1

In El Salvador, _____ parents have a farm. The farm is small and
                2

poor. That is why Estrella and Ana went to the United States.

Estrella and Ana have a brother, Juan. _____ is only 14,
                                        3

and _____ still lives on the farm. _____ wants to go
        4   5

to the United States, too. But Estrella and Ana tell _____ no.
                                                        6

_____ must finish school first.
        7

The sisters also tell _____ that life in the United States is
                        8

not easy. _____ both work very hard. Estrella works all day for a
            9

cleaning company. _____ cleans people's houses and cooks food
                        10

for _____. In the evening, _____ works at a restaurant.
        11   12

In the daytime, Ana works in a hospital. _____ cleans the rooms
                                            13

and helps the patients. In the evening, _____ works at the
                                            14

restaurant, too.

Estrella and Ana want to change _____ lives. Estrella wants
                                    15

to start a small restaurant with Salvadoran food. Ana wants to study to

be a nurse. But now _____ must work hard and put money in
                        16

the bank. Every month _____ also send money to their family in
                        17

El Salvador.

B. *Talk about your answers with another student. Are they the same?*

Relative Pronouns

The relative pronouns *who, which,* and *that* are used to put together two ideas in one sentence.

> **Example:** She's a girl. The girl is in my class.
> She's the girl <u>who</u> is in my class.
> OR She's the girl <u>that</u> is in my class. (more informal)

> **Example:** We ate at the new restaurant. It was very good.
> We ate at the new restaurant, <u>which</u> was very good.

> **Example:** We saw the film. He talked about the film.
> We saw the film <u>that</u> he talked about.

EXAMPLE

Underline the relative pronoun in each sentence. Then write the two ideas as two sentences.

1. We went to Oak Park, <u>which</u> is just outside Chicago.

   We went to Oak Park. Oak Park is just outside Chicago.

2. The dress <u>that</u> I bought is too small.

   I bought a dress. The dress is too small.

> **Note:** You may need to make some small changes in the sentences.
>
> **Example:** the dress → a dress

A. *Underline the relative pronoun in each sentence. Then write the two ideas as two sentences.*

1. Cary showed us the umbrella that she found yesterday.

   _____

2. We don't often see my cousin Betsy, who lives in Seattle.

   _____

3. I have a cat that is all black.

   _____

4. At the party, we met Johanna's husband, who's a basketball player.

   _____

5. We called my father on May 30th, which was his birthday.

   _____

6. Today there was a special sale on the cheese that we like.

   _____

7. I got the jacket from Jane, who doesn't wear it any more.

   _____

8. I read a very good story by Alice Munro that you might like, too.

   _____

B. *Talk about your answers with another student. Are they the same? Then check your answers with your teacher.*

A. *Write the two sentences as one sentence. Use the relative pronoun.*

1. George watched an old movie. It was in French. (which)

2. Today we had a new German teacher. She comes from Berlin. (who)

3. Yesterday I bought some bread. It was very good. (that)

4. The concert is in Framingham. It's outside of Boston. (which)

5. In the hospital, we met an Austrian boy. He spoke English very well. (who)

6. Miriam bought books for her Russian course. It's starting on Monday. (which)

7. I don't think you'll like the Korean film. We saw the film last night. (that)

8. I knew it was Jack. Jack answered the telephone. (who)

B. *Talk about your answers with another student. Are they the same? Then check your answers with your teacher.*

PART

3

Comprehension Skills

Recognizing Letters, Words, and Phrases

When you read, you have to do many things. Your eyes recognize (see and understand) letters and words. This information then goes to your brain. Your brain tries to make sense of the information.

If you are a good reader, you can recognize words very quickly. You don't have to think about the words. You can think about the ideas.

To become a better reader, you need to learn some important skills:
- To recognize letters and words quickly.
- To think about your reading the way good readers do. This will help you find the ideas more easily.

In Part 3, you will learn about and practice these skills.

Recognizing Letters

In these exercises, you will practice recognizing groups of letters. You can find these letters in many English words.

> **Note:** These exercises are not for learning new words. They are for learning to recognize groups of letters. Don't stop to think about each word in the line. Move your eyes fast to look for the key letters.

EXAMPLE

Look for words that __begin__ with the key letters and circle them. Work as quickly as you can.

Key Letters

1. **br**	(bread)	bird	(break)	burn	(bring)
2. **ch**	clean	(cheap)	(child)	class	(cheese)

EXERCISE 1

A. Look for words that _begin_ with the key letters and circle them. Work as quickly as you can.

Key Letters

1.	**sh**	ship	cheap	short	shoe	start
2.	**tw**	twice	town	treasure	twelve	twenty
3.	**gr**	great	group	girl	garden	green
4.	**th**	take	than	talk	that	tall
5.	**cl**	close	chose	clothes	color	clock
6.	**wh**	wait	what	went	wash	when
7.	**pl**	police	place	pool	please	possible
8.	**ch**	chair	clear	case	change	chalk
9.	**st**	shut	store	shirt	start	street
10.	**pr**	person	pretty	present	president	perhaps
11.	**cr**	cross	cry	cost	cows	crowd
12.	**fr**	friend	field	free	fear	fire
13.	**tr**	train	true	turn	their	tree
14.	**wr**	white	write	wrote	word	wrong

B. Look back at the exercise and check your work.

EXERCISE 2

A. Look for words that _begin_ with the key letters and circle them. Work as quickly as you can.

Key Letters

1.	**ba**	bath	both	bank	bag	best
2.	**li**	like	line	life	love	lake
3.	**ta**	table	take	took	taste	teach
4.	**mi**	meal	milk	middle	mail	minute
5.	**fa**	fat	fear	fast	fan	for
6.	**le**	last	let	leg	left	lift
7.	**ho**	hope	home	have	hole	help

8. **bo**	brown	both	born	boat	bone
9. **fe**	feel	feet	face	fear	farm
10. **ha**	head	had	have	happy	heavy
11. **hi**	him	hill	hall	hit	hat
12. **al**	along	alive	afraid	alone	after
13. **ca**	cent	can	carry	cat	chair
14. **do**	daughter	doctor	dollar	dog	drop

B. *Look back at the exercise and check your work.*

EXERCISE 3

A. *Look for words that <u>end</u> with the key letters and circle them. Work as quickly as you can.*

Key Letters

1. **st**	la(st)	mu(st)	ask	co(st)	hurt
2. **ing**	nothing	lesson	during	song	high
3. **ght**	fight	laugh	right	night	white
4. **ful**	careful	chocolate	colorful	beautiful	motorcycle
5. **er**	winter	river	driver	their	were
6. **ly**	while	lovely	loudly	yellow	lightly
7. **ts**	west	wants	pants	parks	starts
8. **et**	fight	forget	biggest	pocket	closet
9. **ld**	child	filled	milk	build	cold
10. **th**	lunch	mouth	bath	wash	north
11. **tch**	match	watch	catch	math	light
12. **rn**	green	learn	burn	farm	born
13. **ese**	Chinese	Japanese	cheese	please	Spanish
14. **ck**	fork	kick	sick	back	like

B. *Look back at the exercise and check your work.*

Recognizing the Sounds of Words

When you read, your eyes recognize letters and words on the page. You also recognize the sounds of these letters and words in spoken English. Knowing how a word sounds helps you understand and remember the word.

In these exercises, you will look for words that rhyme—words that end with the same sound. Sometimes words that rhyme have the same letters, but sometimes they don't. If you don't know a word, make a guess about the way it sounds.

EXAMPLE

Look for the word that does NOT rhyme with the key word and circle it.

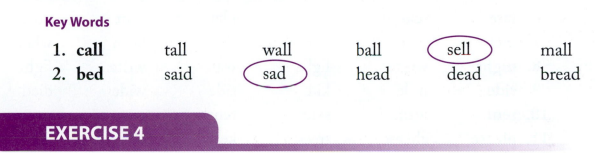

Key Words

| 1. **call** | tall | wall | ball | (sell) | mall |
| 2. **bed** | said | (sad) | head | dead | bread |

EXERCISE 4

A. Work with another student. Say the words aloud. Look for the word that does NOT rhyme with the key word and circle it.

Key Words

1. **will**	bill	hill	kill	still	feel
2. **well**	wheel	sell	tell	smell	spell
3. **near**	wear	beer	year	here	fear
4. **eat**	seat	sweet	cheat	plate	meet
5. **run**	gun	stone	son	fun	one
6. **low**	no	know	show	go	now
7. **bad**	had	mad	sad	dad	paid
8. **game**	ham	came	same	name	fame
9. **not**	pot	spot	hot	boat	got
10. **fat**	sat	hat	eat	cat	that
11. **quick**	like	sick	pick	kick	thick
12. **send**	end	friend	spend	bend	wind
13. **stop**	shop	hope	drop	pop	top
14. **down**	town	own	brown	clown	crown

B. Look back at the exercise and check your work.

A. *Work with another student. Say the words aloud. Look for the word that does NOT rhyme with the key word and circle it.*

Key Words

1. **door**	store	hour	floor	four	more
2. **day**	may	say	grey	buy	way
3. **car**	are	hear	star	far	jar
4. **fruit**	shoot	boot	suit	flute	foot
5. **break**	cake	make	speak	take	steak
6. **late**	seat	date	plate	wait	great
7. **men**	pen	ten	then	been	when
8. **night**	white	light	wait	write	fight
9. **ride**	hide	kid	side	wide	died
10. **rent**	want	sent	tent	went	meant
11. **please**	cheese	trees	keys	these	lies
12. **chair**	wear	dear	pair	hair	care
13. **blue**	zoo	true	you	two	low
14. **me**	free	sea	she	tea	hi

B. *Look back at the exercise and check your work.*

Recognizing Words

The words in Exercises 1–5 are very common. Most of them come from The 100 Words list. (See Part 2, Unit 3, page 80.)

Note: These exercises are not for learning new words. They are for learning to recognize words quickly. Don't stop to think about each word in the line. Move your eyes quickly to look for the key words.

Look for the key word and circle it every time you see it. Work as quickly as you can.

Key Words

1. **into**	onto	unto	(into)	intro	(into)
2. **over**	(over)	aver	ever	our	(over)

EXERCISE 6

A. **Look for the key word and circle it every time you see it. Work as quickly as you can.**

Key Words

1. **out**	out	cut	out	owl	our
2. **make**	mate	mark	make	made	make
3. **back**	black	back	bark	back	bank
4. **that**	hats	than	that	that	treat
5. **gone**	groan	gone	grow	gone	gain
6. **they**	they	they	then	them	they
7. **what**	what	when	white	with	what
8. **then**	them	then	then	than	ten
9. **with**	witch	with	wish	will	with
10. **because**	because	became	because	behave	because
11. **about**	above	abroad	about	about	absorb
12. **time**	time	tine	turn	time	tame
13. **way**	why	way	wax	way	wry
14. **all**	ail	awl	all	add	all
15. **after**	alter	altar	after	afar	offer
16. **been**	been	bean	born	been	barn
17. **write**	white	write	with	white	wait
18. **always**	away	ways	always	already	always

B. **Look back at the exercise and check your work.**

EXERCISE 7

A. *Look for the key word and circle it every time you see it. Work as quickly as you can.*

Key Words

1. **you**	yes	you	yon	yore	you
2. **want**	want	went	ward	wait	want
3. **did**	die	did	dill	dud	dad
4. **fast**	fist	first	fast	fast	fat
5. **head**	head	head	heat	hear	heard
6. **read**	real	reel	read	raid	read
7. **can**	car	can	con	cad	can
8. **was**	war	was	wan	was	wad
9. **any**	any	nay	and	ant	any
10. **are**	art	are	arc	are	air
11. **were**	wear	ware	were	wore	were
12. **two**	tow	two	too	to	two
13. **will**	will	wilt	wall	with	wild
14. **made**	made	made	make	maid	mode
15. **their**	there	these	their	their	three
16. **year**	your	year	yard	yarn	year
17. **day**	dog	day	dad	day	date
18. **most**	most	must	mast	most	mist

B. *Look back at the exercise and check your work.*

A. *Look for the key word and circle it every time you see it. Work as quickly as you can.*

Key Words

1. **have**	hare	have	hive	heave	have
2. **from**	from	from	form	farm	firm
3. **not**	net	not	nut	nod	not
4. **had**	hid	has	had	hat	had
5. **other**	outer	other	order	often	other
6. **some**	soon	same	some	sore	sums
7. **these**	these	three	there	their	those
8. **for**	far	fog	for	fir	four
9. **thought**	though	thought	thorough	thought	through
10. **well**	well	wall	well	will	welt
11. **only**	any	onto	order	only	only
12. **first**	first	forth	first	firmest	fist
13. **letter**	lesson	leader	letter	litter	letter
14. **where**	whether	where	where	when	were
15. **could**	could	course	count	could	couple
16. **would**	would	worth	world	wound	would
17. **even**	ever	eleven	even	earn	even
18. **but**	bud	but	bust	bit	but

B. *Look back at the exercise and check your work.*

EXERCISE 9

A. Look for the key word and circle it every time you see it. Work as quickly as you can.

Key Words

1. **people**	pepper	penny	people	period	people
2. **like**	lake	leak	like	lite	like
3. **most**	mast	must	mist	moat	most
4. **who**	won	who	why	wok	who
5. **right**	ridge	rigid	right	right	night
6. **year**	year	year	yeah	your	yarn
7. **this**	thin	these	thus	this	this
8. **more**	more	more	mare	mode	move
9. **hot**	not	net	hot	hat	hot
10. **now**	new	none	not	now	nod
11. **him**	him	his	him	hit	hill
12. **good**	gold	good	guard	gone	good
13. **when**	where	when	wean	when	were
14. **save**	save	same	sale	saws	save
15. **call**	calf	cell	call	call	calm
16. **busy**	bury	bush	busy	bust	busy
17. **week**	week	weak	week	weed	weep
18. **have**	hare	haze	have	hive	have

B. Look back at the exercise and check your work.

Recognizing Phrases

Some phrases (groups of words) are often used together. You can read faster if you learn and read these words together. In these exercises you will practice scanning for key phrases.

Some Common Kinds of Phrases

Verb + preposition (phrasal verb): He was tired, so he <u>sat down</u>.

Prepositional phrase: There was a park <u>at the end</u> of the street.

Adverbial phrase: The bus is never <u>on time</u>.

Note: These exercises are not for learning new phrases. They are for learning to recognize phrases quickly. Don't stop to think about each phrase in the line. Move your eyes quickly to look for the key phrases.

EXERCISE 10

A. *Look for the key phrase and circle it every time you see it. Work as quickly as you can.*

Key Phrases

1. **get up**	get in	set up	get up	go up
	get up	got in	get up	get out
2. **fall down**	fall dead	feel down	fast down	fall down
	feel dark	fall down	fell down	fall down
3. **look for**	like our	look at	look for	look far
	look for	look four	lord of	long for
4. **turn off**	turn on	true one	turn off	time off
	turn off	time off	turn out	turn off
5. **run away**	ran away	run away	run around	run about
	run any	ran always	run away	ran after
6. **get down**	get dinner	got down	get dry	get down
	got dark	get down	get brown	get known

7. **wait for**	wait for	wake for	wait far	want few
	wet food	wait for	what for	wait for
8. **come back**	come buy	come back	came back	come daily
	some bark	come bake	come back	came before

B. *Look back at the exercise and check your work.*

A. *Look for the key phrase and circle it every time you see it. Work as quickly as you can.*

Key Phrases

1. **by car**	buy car	by car	by cab	by car
	by car	but call	boy cat	my car
2. **on top of**	into the	on top of	in touch	a pot of
	on this	or twice	on top of	the top of
3. **a lot of**	a lot of	a little	a list of	a long
	a lost one	a life of	a lot of	a loaf of
4. **of course**	on course	of course	if curious	our cousin
	of course	of coffee	on cloth	of course
5. **in front of**	in favor of	in front of	in from	in the flow
	in front of	in front of	in the font of	on the floor
6. **on the way**	on the wane	or the way	on the way	in the way
	in the war	on the way	on their way	on the wall
7. **for example**	for expense	for evening	for example	far exceed
	far example	for every	for example	for example
8. **in the world**	in the word	of the world	in the world	in the works
	in the world	in the way	in the wild	if the word

B. *Look back at the exercise and check your work.*

EXERCISE 12

A. *Look for the key phrase and circle it every time you see it. Work as quickly as you can.*

Key Phrases

1. **how much**	how much have men	have many have money	how many how mean	hot meal how much
2. **far away**	far along for a war	for a way far across	far away far around	for a wait far away
3. **last year**	last day last yard	fast year last year	last year last girl	less fear late year
4. **all the time**	at the time all the term	at the table at the term	as the trip and the time	all the time as the tide
5. **at last**	at least a lack	at last as last	at large at last	at loss are last
6. **once again**	once upon one agent	one again once agree	one age once again	one angry one angel
7. **next door**	new door next dozen	next day next door	next door never done	new draw news day
8. **on time**	on line on time	on time in line	in time on tour	on mine on time

B. *Look back at the exercise and check your work.*

Focus on Vocabulary

A. *Do you know the meanings of these words? Read each word aloud. Then put a ✓ (you know), ? (you aren't sure), or X (you don't know).*

_____ successful	_____ smart	_____ funny
_____ tax	_____ (in) trouble	_____ popular
_____ interested (in)	_____ violent	_____ earn

B. *Read the passage to the end.*

Will Smith—Part 1

First, he was a very good hip-hop singer. Then he was successful on television. And finally, he became a famous movie star. Who is he? Will Smith, an African American, and one of the best-paid actors in Hollywood.

His full name is Willard Christopher Smith, Jr. He was born in 1968
5   in Philadelphia. His mother worked for the schools and his father was an engineer. In high school, he was very popular. His friends called him "Prince." He was also very smart, but he didn't get good grades. He wasn't interested in schoolwork. He liked to talk and spend time with his friends. And he loved music.

10   When he was only 12, he began to rap. This is a kind of very fast talking to music. Will was very good at this. At 16, he met Jeff Townes, and they began to make music together. They were called "DJ Jazzy Jeff and the Fresh Prince." The words to their songs weren't dirty and violent like some rap songs. They were clean and funny. In 1986, they had their first big hit. Then they had an
15   even bigger hit in 1989 with the song "Parents Just Don't Understand."

Will and Jeff earned a lot of money with their songs. By the time he was 18, Will was already a millionaire. But the money didn't stay in his pockets for long. He was young, and there were lots of ways to spend it. He was also in trouble with the government because he didn't pay taxes.

C. *Look back at the passage and circle the words from the list in part A. (Some words may be in a different form: earn → earned, tax → taxes.) Then underline the words you don't know.*

D. *Look up the underlined words in the dictionary and write them in your vocabulary notebook. (See Part 2, Unit 1, page 71.)*

E. *Check your understanding of the passage. Read it again if you need to. Write T (true) or F (false) after each sentence.*

_____ 1. Will came from a poor family.

_____ 2. He liked music better than schoolwork.

_____ 3. Will and Jeff's rap songs were not dirty.

_____ 4. Will and Jeff made a lot of money.

F. *Talk about your answers with another student. Are they the same? Then check all your work with your teacher.*

EXERCISE 14

A. *Read each sentence and circle the best meaning for the underlined word(s).*

1. Then, he was <u>successful</u> on television.
   a. happy   b. famous   c. often

2. In high school, he was <u>very popular</u>.
   a. liked a lot   b. helped a lot   c. hurt a lot

3. He was also <u>very smart</u>, but he didn't get good grades.
   a. a good thinker   b. a good runner   c. a good driver

4. He <u>wasn't interested in</u> schoolwork.
   a. liked doing   b. couldn't do   c. didn't want to do

5. The words to their songs weren't dirty and <u>violent</u> like some rap songs.
   a. difficult   b. sad   c. aggressive

6. They were clean and <u>funny</u>.
   a. made you laugh   b. easy to sing   c. told about love

7. Will and Jeff <u>earned</u> a lot of money with their songs.
   a. lost   b. got   c. spent

8. He <u>was also in trouble with</u> the government because he didn't pay taxes.
   a. also had problems with
   b. was also paid by
   c. was also working for

9. He was also in trouble with the government because he didn't pay <u>taxes</u>.
   a. money for his family
   b. money for the government
   c. money for things he bought

B. *Talk about your answers with another student. Are they the same?*

EXERCISE 15

A. *Complete the sentences with the words from the box. Use each word only once. Change the word for the sentence if necessary (plural, past tense, etc.).*

successful	smart	violent	earn	tax
popular	interested (in)	funny	(in) trouble	

1. George is _____ with the teacher because he didn't do his homework.

2. The new teacher was not very _____ with the children. They didn't like him much.

3. He was a _____ little boy. He could read and write very well.

4. Our friend Iannis is very _____. He always makes us laugh.

5. A doctor _____ a lot more than a nurse.

6. Every year we have to pay _____ to the city and to the state.

7. Professor Smith is _____ early American history.

8. Bill Gates is a very _____ businessman.

9. I didn't watch the _____ parts of the movie. I don't like to see people get hurt.

B. *Talk about your answers with another student. Are they the same?*

EXERCISE 16

A. *Write a sentence for each word in the box. Look at the sentences in Exercises 14 and 15 if you need help.*

successful	smart	violent	earn	tax
popular	interested (in)	funny	(in) trouble	

1. _____
2. _____
3. _____
4. _____
5. _____
6. _____
7. _____
8. _____
9. _____

B. *Check your work with your teacher.*

EXERCISE 17

A. *Write the other parts of speech for each word. More than one answer is possible. (See Part 2, Unit 5, page 100.)*

1. **tax** (n)   verb: _____

2. **violent** (adj)   noun: _____

3. **successful** (adj)   adverb: _____

          noun: _____

          verb: _____

(continued)

4. funny (adj)   adjective (another form): _____

                                   noun: _____

5. interested (adj) adjective (another form): _____

                                   noun: _____

                                   verb: _____

B. *Talk about your answers with another student. Are they the same? Then check your answers with your teacher.*

C. *Write all the new words from Exercises 13–17 in your vocabulary notebook. Then make study cards. Study them alone and then with another student.*

Scanning

What Is Scanning?

- It's very fast reading.

When Do You Scan?

- You scan when you want to find information quickly.
- You scan a list, an advertisement, a webpage, or a newspaper article.

How Do You Scan?

- You move your eyes very quickly over the page.
- You don't read all the words.
- You read only the words that help you find the information.

Scanning exercises help you learn to find information fast. This is often useful in everyday life, at work, and at school. These exercises also help you learn to move your eyes quickly. This will make you a better reader.

In this unit, you will scan for information. In each exercise, there are questions. Scan the graphic or passage to find the answers.

> *Note:* You don't need to read or understand everything in these exercises. You only need to look for the words that help you answer the questions.

A. *Scan the marathon results on page 139 for the answers to the questions. Work as quickly as you can.*

1. Where did the winner come from?

   _____

2. What were the places of the two Kenyan runners?

   _____

3. What was the time for Paula Radcliffe?

   _____

4. What was place of the Ethiopian runner?

   _____

5. Who ran with bib number F1?

   _____

6. What state did the 12th place runner come from?

   _____

7. What was the time for the French runner?

   _____

8. How many Americans were in the first 15 places?

   _____

B. *Write three more questions about the results. Then ask another student to scan for the answers.*

_____

_____

_____

C. *Talk with another student. Ask and answer these questions.*

1. Are your answers to part A the same?
2. Do you like to run? Do you know any runners?
3. Do you like sports? If so, what sports?

2007 New York City Marathon Results (Women)

Place	Bib	Name	Time	Country	State
1	F2	Paula Radcliffe	2:23:09	Great Britain	
2	F4	Gete Wami	2:23:32	Ethiopia	
3	F1	Jelena Prokopcuka	2:26:13	Latvia	
4	F5	Lidiya Grigoryeva	2:28:37	Russia	
5	F3	Caterine Ndereba	2:29:08	Kenya	
6	F10	Elva Dryer	2:35:15	USA	Colorado
7	F20	Robyn Friedman	2:39:19	USA	Iowa
8	F11	Tegla Loroupe	2:42:58	Kenya	
9	F37	Melisa Christian	2:42:07	USA	Texas
10	F27	Alvina Begay	2:42:46	USA	Arizona
11	F17	Christine Lundy	2:43:21	USA	California
12	F19	Veena Reddy	2:43:26	USA	Pennsylvania
13	F33	Caitlin Tormey	2:43:30	USA	New York
14	F16	Erin Moeller	2:43:57	USA	Iowa
15	F42	Nathalie Vasseur	2:44:00	France	

A. *Scan the concert calendar on page 141 for the answers to the questions. Work as quickly as you can.*

1. Which place has the cheapest tickets?
_____

2. On what dates can you see B.B. King?
_____

3. What time is the John Prine concert?
_____

4. What kind of music does Alejandro Escovedo play?
_____

5. Who can you see on Sunday, December 6?
_____

6. Who plays Latin Jazz?
_____

7. Who can you see at the Grant Auditorium?
_____

8. On which dates can you see the St. Louis All-Star Band?
_____

B. *Write three more questions about the concert calendar. Then ask another student to scan for the answers.*

_____
_____
_____

C. *Talk with another student. Ask and answer these questions.*

1. Are your answers to part A the same?
2. Do you like to listen to music? If so, what kind of music do you listen to?
3. Do you ever go to concerts? If so, tell about some concerts you went to.

Concert CALENDAR

Concert	Date	Time	Ticket Price	Place	Type of Music
B.B. King	Friday, December 4	7:30	$35	Hartz Hall	Blues
John Prine	Friday, December 4	8:30	$10	Club Café	Folk
The Clarks	Friday, December 4	8:00	$15	The Roadhouse	Rock
B.B. King	Saturday, December 5	8:00	$35	Hartz Hall	Blues
Chris Smither	Saturday, December 5	7:30	$27	Grant Auditorium	Folk/Blues
All Things Indie	Saturday, December 5	10:00	$12	Homer Tavern	Dance & DJ
Emmylou Harris	Sunday, December 6	7:00	$37	Duke Theater	Country/Folk
Alejandro Escovedo	Sunday, December 6	8:00	$28	Club Café	Rock/Country
Arturo O'Farrill	Sunday, December 6	7:30	$26	The Roadhouse	Latin Jazz
Debbie Davies	Monday, December 7	8:00	$27	Duke Theater	Blues
St. Louis All-Star Band	Monday, December 7	7:00	$17	Hartz Hall	Jazz/Holiday
Alvin Jett Duo	Tuesday, December 8	9:00	$12	Homer Tavern	Jazz/Blues

A. *Scan the list of books on page 143 for the answers to the questions. Work as quickly as you can.*

1. Who is the author of *Lucky Break*?

    _____

2. Which book is about ancient Egypt?

    _____

3. Which books were written by Stephen Rabley?

    _____

4. Who are the authors of the book about Tina Daniels?

    _____

5. Which book is about the Pyncheon family?

    _____

6. Which book is about a basketball player?

    _____

7. Which books are biographies (about real people)?

    _____

8. Where are the people in *The Big Bag Mistake*?

    _____

B. *Write three more questions about the list of books. Then ask another student to scan for the answers.*

_____

_____

_____

C. *Talk with another student. Ask and answer these questions.*

1. Are your answers to part A the same?
2. Are any of these books interesting to you? If so, why?
3. What kinds of books do you like best?

Extensive Reading Books

The Big Bag Mistake. Escott, John. Ricardo and Gisela are going home to Rio in Brazil. Gisela likes reading and quiet people. Ricardo likes noise . . . and he likes Gisela. In Rio, a thief takes Gisela's bag. What can Ricardo do?

Daniel Radcliffe. Shipton, Vicky. We all know Daniel Radcliffe's face from the Harry Potter films. But how did he get the job? Did he always want to be an actor? And what did he do before Harry Potter? This is the story of young Daniel's life.

The Fireboy. Rabley, Stephen. Hapu lives in ancient Egypt. He works for his father, a goldsmith. One day Hapu has a wonderful idea. He will make a beautiful gold necklace for Queen Cleopatra.

The House of the Seven Gables. Hawthorne, Nathaniel. The House of the Seven Gables is the home of an important family: the Pyncheons. They have the house and a lot of land, but no money and many problems. Is there a curse on the family? This is a classic story about money, murder, and love.

Lucky Break. Escott, John. Tom breaks his leg in a football game—it's not his lucky day! A week later, Tom sees his favorite movie star. But Tom falls again—and suddenly the movie star is falling, too! Reporters are taking pictures of Tom. Is this his lucky break?

Maisie and the Dolphin. Rabley, Stephen. Maisie King lives in the Bahamas. Her mother and father work at an animal hospital. Maisie has a new friend. His name is Ben, and he's a dolphin. Ben is very ill. Maisie helps him. Then Maisie has a big problem. Can Ben help her?

Michael Jordan. Taylor, Nancy. Michael Jordan, the Chicago Bulls' number 23, is very famous. And he can fly! Maybe he is the best basketball player of all time. But where did he come from? How did he start in basketball? Read about his life and about his love of basketball.

The Pearl Girl. Rabley, Stephen. Kate Grant comes from Canada. She is visiting Europe with her mother and father. One evening she sees two men in a museum. They are taking a very famous picture, Girl with a Pearl Earring. What can Kate do?

Tom Cruise. Smith, Rod. One of Hollywood's most successful actors, Tom Cruise has starred in numerous films since his debut in Risky Business. Read about his life and career, his major film roles, his involvement with Scientology, and his marriages.

Who Wants to be a Star? Allen, Julia and Iggulden, Margaret. Tina Daniels sings beautifully, and her mother has big ideas about Hollywood, but Tina is not happy. One day she goes away on a train. Who does she meet? What does she see?

A. Scan the article on page 145 for the answers to the questions. (Remember, you don't need to read all the words.) Work as quickly as you can.

1. What years did the authors review for the research?

   _____

2. Who led the researchers?

   _____

3. How many people were riding in police cars?

   _____

4. How many people died?

   _____

5. What percent of them were not wearing seat belts?

   _____

6. What journal was the report in?

   _____

7. What university does Jehle work for?

   _____

8. What percent of the deaths happened during routine driving?

   _____

B. Talk with another student. Ask and answer these questions.

1. Are your answers to part A the same?
2. What laws does your country have about seat belts?
3. Do you always use a seat belt?

Unbelted and at Risk

More police officers die each year in car crashes than at the hands of criminals. Most of the time, the accidents happen during routine driving, not when the officers are speeding to an emergency.

A new study says there would be fewer deaths if police officers used seat belts more. The report was published in The Journal of Trauma. In their research, the authors reviewed hundreds of police car accidents across America from 1997 to 2001. They learned that officers in crashes were 2.6 times more likely to die if they didn't wear seat belts.

The researchers were led by Dietrich von Kuenssberg Jehle, researcher at the University of Buffalo School of Medicine and Biomedical Sciences. The study looked at 516 people who were riding in police cars during accidents. In all, 106 of them died. About 40 percent of those who died were not wearing seat belts, the study said.

Jehle said that officers in the study were surprised to find that about 60 percent of the deaths happened during routine driving. Officers tend to think that speeding to an emergency is far more dangerous.

(adapted from IHT 3/2/05)

A. *Scan the article on page 147 for the answers to the questions. (Remember, you don't need to read all the words.) Work as quickly as you can.*

1. How tall is the Sears Tower?

   _____

2. What other U.S. cities are in the article?

   _____

3. What city has the most skyscrapers?

   _____

4. Where are the Petronas towers?

   _____

5. What will soon be the tallest skyscraper in the United States?

   _____

6. What is the name of the building in Dubai?

   _____

7. When was the first skyscraper built?

   _____

8. What was completed in 1972?

   _____

B. *Talk with another student. Ask and answer these questions.*

1. Are your answers to part A the same?
2. Are there any tall buildings in your hometown or city?
3. Would you like to live or work in a tall building? Why or why not?

Scraping the Sky

Chicago is well known for its skyscrapers. In fact, it was there that the first skyscraper was built in 1885. The Home Insurance Building was only 11 stories high, but for the first time, steel was used in the building. The use of steel made it possible to build higher and higher.

Other cities, such as Boston and New York, also built skyscrapers in the late 19th century and early 20th century. In New York, there was a big competition for the tallest building. It was won by the Empire State Building in 1931. This was the tallest building in New York and in the world until the World Trade Center was completed in 1972.

Today Chicago is not the only U.S. city with plans for new skyscrapers. Other cities are also going to build towers, including New York, Miami, San Francisco, and Las Vegas. In New York, the Freedom Tower will go up in place of the Twin Towers. It will be the tallest building in the city at 1,776 feet (541 meters), but not as tall as the Fordham Tower in Chicago.

All around the world, buildings are going higher. After September 11, 2001, many people were afraid of tall buildings. They were afraid that terrorists could make the buildings fall down like the Twin Towers in New York. But that soon changed. Now in the United States and in Asia, many cities are planning new skyscrapers.

In the United States, Chicago now has the tallest building in the country, the Sears Tower, at 1,450 feet (442 meters). This is also one of the tallest buildings in the world. Several other tall buildings will be built in Chicago. One of these is the Fordham Tower, which will soon be the tallest building in the country, at 115 stories or 2,000 feet (610 meters).

Worldwide, the city with the most skyscrapers is Hong Kong. It has more than New York or Chicago. Buildings of 60 stories are very common in Hong Kong, for both offices and apartments. Until a short time ago, the highest building in the world was in Malaysia—the Petronas Towers, 1,483 feet (452 meters). Then, in 2007, a taller building was built in Taipei—the Taipei 101, 1,667 feet (508 meters). But the highest building in the world will soon be the Burj Tower in Dubai, at about 2,300 feet (701 meters).

Focus on Vocabulary

A. *Do you know the meanings of these words? Read each word aloud. Then put a ✓ (you know), ? (you aren't sure), or X (you don't know).*

____ prize	____ career	____ relative
____ naturally	____ private	____ continue
____ teenage	____ joke	____ several
____ careful		

B. *Read the passage to the end.*

Will Smith—Part 2

After Will paid all his taxes to the government, he had no money. But this was not a problem. He and Jeff soon had more big hits. In 1989 and in 1991, they got an important prize (a Grammy Award) for their songs.

5 For the next few years, Will continued to write rap songs and make videos. But he also started another career. In 1990, some television writers asked him to be in a show. In fact, he was the star of the program. It was called *The Fresh Prince of Bel-Air.*

The show was about a teenage boy from Philadelphia (like his real life). This boy goes to live with rich relatives in Bel-Air, a part of Los Angeles. He 10 is always laughing and telling jokes. But his aunt, uncle, and cousins are very serious. Naturally, there are lots of problems, but in the end, everyone loves him. The show was a huge success for six years.

While he was still on the show, Will Smith also began his movie career. He had small parts in several movies in the early 1990s. His first big part came 15 in 1996 in the movie *Independence Day.* After that, he was in many important movies. Some of them were *Men in Black; Bad Boys; Ali; I, Robot; The Pursuit of Happyness;* and *I Am Legend.*

In his private life, Will Smith likes to live quietly. He was married to Sheree Zampino from 1992–1995. They had a son, Willard Smith III. Then 20 he married Jada Pinkett in 1997. They have a son, Jaden, and a daughter, Willow. As a top movie star, Will Smith is a very rich man. But he is more careful about his money now, and he pays his taxes!

C. Look back at the passage and circle the words from the list in part A. (Some words may be in a different form: continue → continued.) Then underline all of the words you don't know.

D. Look up the underlined words in the dictionary and write them in your vocabulary notebook. (See Part 2, Unit 1, page 71.)

E. Check your understanding of the passage. Read it again if you need to. Write T (true) or F (false) before each sentence.

_____ 1. *The Fresh Prince of Bel-Air* was about a boy like Will.

_____ 2. He sang rap songs on the television program.

_____ 3. Will's movie career began after the year 1999.

_____ 4. Will has three children.

F. Talk about your answers with another student. Are they the same? Then check all your work with your teacher.

EXERCISE 7

A. Read each sentence and circle the best meaning for the underlined word(s).

1. In 1989 and in 1991, they got an important <u>prize</u> (a Grammy Award) for their songs.
   a. something you make
   b. something you buy
   c. something you win

2. For the next few years, Will <u>continued to write</u> rap songs, and he made more videos.
   a. wrote more
   b. listened to more
   c. stopped writing

3. But he also started another <u>career</u>.
   a. way to make music
   b. small business
   c. kind of job

4. The show was about a <u>teenage</u> boy from Philadelphia (like his real life).
   a. 13- to 19-year-old
   b. 22-year-old
   c. 10- to 12-year-old

5. This boy goes to live with rich <u>relatives</u> in Bel-Air, a part of Los Angeles.
   a. families of movie stars
   b. people in his family
   c. friends of his family

6. He is always laughing and telling <u>jokes</u>.
   a. long stories
   b. loud stories
   c. funny stories

7. <u>Naturally</u>, there are lots of problems, but in the end everyone loves him.
   a. After a while
   b. Of course
   c. Soon

8. He had small parts in <u>several</u> movies in the early 1990s.
   a. one
   b. seven
   c. a few

9. In his <u>private</u> life, Will Smith likes to live quietly.
   a. show
   b. business
   c. home

10. But he <u>is more careful about</u> his money now and he pays his taxes!
    a. thinks more about
    b. spends more of
    c. buys more with

B. *Talk about your answers with another student. Are they the same?*

EXERCISE 8

A. *Complete the sentences with the words from the box. Use each word only once. Change the word for the sentence if necessary (plural, past tense, etc.).*

prize	career	relative	naturally	private
continue	teenage	joke	several	careful

1. She began a new _____ when she was 50 years old.

2. Many people write about their _____ lives on Internet.

3. He was very _____ not to make mistakes on the test.

4. Professor Jones will _____ to work at the university next year.

5. She won the _____ for the best book of short stories.

6. _____, Sula wanted to win the race.

7. Everyone was surprised when the president told a _____.

8. I tried to call you _____ times last night.

9. She's going to visit her _____ in the south of Italy.

10. This kind of music is for _____ girls.

B. **Talk about your answers with another student. Are they the same?**

EXERCISE 9

A. *Write a sentence for each word in the box. Look at the sentences in Exercises 7 and 8 if you need help.*

prize	career	relative	naturally	private
continue	teenage	joke	several	careful

1. _____

2. _____

3. _____

4. _____

5. _____

6. _____

7. _____

8. _____

9. _____

10. _____

B. **Check your work with your teacher.**

A. *Write the other parts of speech for each word. More than one answer is possible. (See Part 2, Unit 5, page 100.)*

1. **teenage** (adj)   noun: _____

2. **private** (adj)   adverb: _____
                              noun: _____

3. **naturally** (adv)   adjective: _____
                              noun: _____

4. **continue** (verb)   noun: _____
                              adjective: _____
                              adverb: _____

5. **careful** (adj)   adverb: _____
                              noun: _____
                              verb: _____

B. *Talk about your answers with another student. Are they the same? Then check your answers with your teacher.*

C. *Write all the new words from Exercises 6–10 in your vocabulary notebook. Then make study cards. Study them alone and then with another student.*

Making Inferences

How Do You Make Inferences?

An inference is a kind of guess. When you see a picture or read a passage, you get information from it. Then you can guess (make an inference) about other things that are not in the picture or passage.

When Do You Make Inferences?

In everyday life, you often make inferences. For example:

- One morning, you are listening to the news on the radio. You hear that there was an accident on Route 6. You make an inference from this:

    There will be bad traffic on Route 6. You should take another road today.

- You read in the newspaper about a new bridge between Shanghai and Ningbo in China. This bridge (23 miles/35 km) is the longest bridge in the world. You make an inference from this:

    There is water—probably the sea—between Shanghai and Ningbo.

Good readers also make inferences. For example:

- Sometimes not all the information is complete in a passage.

    Readers make inferences about the missing information. Then they can understand better.

- Sometimes there are new words in a passage.

    Readers make inferences about the general meaning of these words. This way they can understand the passage and keep reading. (See Part 2, Unit 4, page 87.)

In this unit, you will practice making inferences when you are reading.

Making Inferences from Pictures

In these exercises, you will make inferences from pictures.

EXERCISE 1

A. *Look at the picture. Make inferences to answer the questions.*

1. Where are these people? _____
2. What are they doing? _____
3. What are they saying? _____
4. How do they feel? _____

B. *Talk about your answers with another student. Are they the same?*

Riddles

In these exercises, you will make inferences to answer riddles.

EXERCISE 2

A. *These riddles are about food. Read them and make inferences to answer the questions.*

1. It's brown.
   You can drink it.
   You can put milk or sugar in it.
   It isn't tea.

   What is it? _____

2. It's orange.
   It's often long and thin.
   It's good before it's cooked.
   It's good cooked.

   What is it? _____

3. It's white.
   It's sweet.
   You can put it in coffee or tea.
   You often use it in cakes.

   What is it? _____

4. It's white.
   It's not sweet.
   You can put it on meat or vegetables.
   You don't put it in coffee.

   What is it? _____

5. It can be red, green, or yellow.
   It comes from a tree.
   You can eat it from the tree.
   You can cook it, too.

   What is it? _____

B. *Talk about your answers with another student. Are they the same?*

A. *These riddles are about animals. Read them and make inferences to answer the questions.*

1. It lives on a farm.
   It eats grass.
   It usually stays in groups.
   People make warm clothes from its hair.

   What is it? _____

2. It's very, very big.
   It lives in the ocean.
   It needs to come up to get air.
   The baby drinks milk from its mother.

   What is it? _____

3. It can jump far.
   It sleeps a lot.
   It makes a soft noise when it's happy.
   Many people have one in their homes.

   What is it? _____

4. It lives in most places around the world.
   It's small and gray.
   It has a long tail.
   Some people are afraid of it.

   What is it? _____

5. It's very small, and it can fly.
   It's not very clean.
   It goes on food or on other animals.
   People try to kill it.

   What is it? _____

B. *Talk about your answers with another student. Are they the same?*

A. *These riddles are about people at work. Read them and make inferences to answer the questions.*

1. They leave for work in the evening.
   They come home in the morning.
   They are on their feet all night.
   Most of the time, nothing happens.
   Sometimes they have to call the police.

   What are they? _____

2. They go to many places around the world.
   Sometimes there are wars or dangerous weather.
   They talk to people in these places.
   Then they tell about it to the people at home.
   Many people watch them on TV.

   What are they? _____

3. They sit up high.
   At the same time, they move around the city.
   They go to many places every day.
   They see many different people.
   The people pay to go with them.

   What are they? _____

4. They have the best office in the building.
   They have meetings in restaurants.
   They make lots of telephone calls.
   They travel a lot.
   They work very long hours.

   What are they? _____

5. They wait for many hours or days.
   They clean the trucks.
   Then a call comes, and they move fast.
   Their job can be dangerous.
   They save lives.

   What are they? _____

B. *Talk about your answers with another student. Are they the same?*

Making Inferences from Conversations

In these exercises, you will make inferences about the people in the conversations.

EXAMPLE

Read the conversation. Make inferences to answer the questions.

A: Does that hurt?
B: Ow! Yes it does!
A: Can you move it at all?
B: Only a little.
A: Can you walk on it?
B: No. It hurts too much.
A: I think we need to take X-rays.

1. Where are these people? *In a doctor's office.*
2. Who are they? *A is a doctor, and B is a patient.*
3. What are they talking about? *B hurt his/her leg. A thinks it could be broken.*

Note: For some questions, there is more than one possible answer. Your answer is good if you can explain it.

EXERCISE 5

A. *Read the conversation. Make inferences to answer the questions.*

A: What do you think?
B: The color's great.
A: It's very red.
B: We also have it in blue with short sleeves.
A: No, I like red. But maybe I'm too old for this.
B: Of course not.

1. Where are these people? _____
2. Who are they? _____
3. What are they talking about? _____

B. *Talk about your answers with another student. Are they the same? Then check your answers with your teacher.*

EXERCISE 6

A. *Read the conversation. Make inferences to answer the questions.*

A: Oh, no! Look at that line.
B: That's for the security check.
A: We only have 20 minutes!
B: The line's moving.
A: But it's a long way to our gate.
B: It's okay. We'll be fine.

1. Where are these people? _____

2. Who are they? _____

3. How does each person feel? _____

B. *Talk about your answers with another student. Are they the same? Then check your answers with your teacher.*

EXERCISE 7

A. *Read the conversation. Make inferences to answer the questions.*

A: Are you waiting for Professor Small?
B: Yeah. Do you know him?
A: I had him last year for American Lit.
B: I'm taking that course now. He sure makes you write a lot of papers! I'm not so good at writing papers, so I thought I'd talk to him.
A: Why don't you go to the Writing Center? They'll help you.
B: The Writing Center? That's a great idea. Thanks.
A: No problem. Maybe I'll see you there sometime.

1. Where are these people? _____

2. Who are they? _____

3. Why is B there? _____

4. What will B probably do next? _____

B. *Talk with another student about your answers. Are they the same? Then check your answers with your teacher.*

A. *Read the conversation. Make inferences to answer the questions.*

A: For here or to go?

B: For here. Do you have anything that isn't fried?

A: How about grilled chicken?

B: No, I don't want chicken. Don't you have anything else?

A: Well, we have . . . ah . . . hot dogs.

B: Hmm. No, I think I'll have the chicken.

A. Okay . . . Do you want fries with that?

B: No, nothing fried!

A. Oh, yeah. Sorry. We've got salad, mixed salad.

B: All right, I guess that's okay.

A: Anything to drink?

B: Can I have some water?

A: Ah. Yeah, sure. Here's a cup. You can get some water over there.

1. Where are these people? _____

2. Who are they? _____

3. What type of food does B prefer to eat? _____

4. What does A probably think about B? _____

B. *Talk about your answers with another student. Are they the same? Then check your answers with your teacher.*

Making Inferences from Stories

In each of these exercises, there is a passage from a book. You will make inferences from the passage about the people in the story.

For some questions, there is more than one possible answer. Your answer is okay if you can explain it with words from the story.

A. *Read the passage from* **Mike's Lucky Day** *by Leslie Dunkling. Make inferences to answer the questions.*

Mike and Bill go to Morgan's in the afternoon, and Jennifer is there again.
"You're right, Mike," Bill says. "Jennifer *has* got beautiful eyes! And Mike likes your hair," Bill says to Jennifer.
Jennifer looks at Mike. His face is red. "Lucky me!" she says, and she
5 laughs.
Mike can't look at her. "Bill, I can't find those cans of cheese," he says.
"Cans of cheese? What cans of cheese?"
"The cans of cheese for Morgan's," Mike says. "I can't find them."
"Mike, we don't have cheese for Morgan's. We have *peas*—cans of *peas*."
10 Bill and Jennifer laugh again. Mike goes to the van and comes in again with the peas.
He puts the box on the counter. "Here are your peas," he says to Jennifer. His face is red again.
Jennifer smiles at him. "Thank you," she says. She has a beautiful smile.

1. Where are these people? _____

2. What is Mike's job? _____

3. What is Jennifer's job? _____

4. Why does Mike's face turn red? _____

B. *Talk with another student about your answers. Are they the same? Then check your answers with your teacher.*

A. *Read the passage from* **The Battle of Newton Road** *by Leslie Dunkling. Make inferences to answer the questions.*

"We're going to stay in Newton Road," Sally says. "Mr. Wood can't build a new road. Newton Road is our road. This is a battle—the battle of Newton Road."

It is Monday. Sally Robson is at school. She tells her students about the
5   meeting. She tells them about Mr. Wood and the new road.

"He can't build a new road here," they say. "He can't knock down the houses and our school."

But Mr. Wood is a clever man. He shows the new houses to Helen Taylor. He shows them to Paul Johnson.

10   "Mr. Wood isn't a bad man," Helen Taylor tells Sally. "And the new houses aren't bad."

"They're very good," Paul Johnson says. "And they have big gardens. Think about that."

1. What is Sally Robson's job? _____

2. What is Mr. Wood's job? _____

3. Why is there a "battle"? _____

4. Who agrees with Sally? _____

B. *Talk with another student about your answers. Are they the same? Then check your answers with your teacher.*

A. *Read the passage from* **Tinker's Farm** *by Stephen Rabley. Make inferences to answer the questions.*

Four days later, Jenny and Blue Sky are making the beds. Suddenly they hear something. Two men are shouting. Jenny looks out of the window. She can see Jack Crane and her father in front of the farmhouse. Jack Crane's face is very red.

5 "Do it!" he shouts.

"No, I'm not going to do it!" Sam shouts back. "It's Sunday, and I don't work on Sundays. *You* do it!"

Jenny runs downstairs and out of the house. There is a strong wind, and it is raining.

10 "What's happening?" she asks her father.

"We're leaving in the morning," Sam answers. He is walking very fast. Jenny looks at him.

"But . . . how are we going to *eat*? We don't have any money."

Sam does not answer. His eyes are cold and hard.

1. Where are the people? _____

2. What does Jack Crane want? _____

3. Why are Sam's eyes cold and hard? _____

4. What does Jenny think? _____

B. *Talk about your answers with another student. Are they the same? Then check your answers with your teacher.*

A. *Read the passage from* **Island for Sale** *by Anne Collins. Make inferences to answer the questions.*

Leaping Larry says, "We want to see the island."

"All right," says Duncan. "We can go in my boat."

Duncan, Larry, and Roxanne get into Duncan's boat. Jock jumps in, too. Roxanne is carrying Bobo.

5 Duncan takes them around the island. The sun is shining, and it's a beautiful day. But Roxanne isn't happy.

"What do you do all day?" she asks Duncan.

(continued)

"Well," says Duncan. "I go for walks and I fish. And sometimes I go swimming."

10   "Is that all?" Roxanne asks.

"Well," says Duncan, "I'm also writing a book."

"A book!" says Roxanne. "That isn't very exciting."

"Listen, honey," says Larry. "We can make the island exciting. We can have pop concerts here. It's just fine for concerts. Hundreds of people can come!"

15   Duncan looks at Jock. Jock looks at Duncan.

"Pop concerts!" they think. "Oh, no!"

1. Where are the people? _____

2. Where does Duncan live? _____

3. Does Roxanne like the island? Why or why not? _____

_____

4. What does Duncan think about Leaping Larry and Roxanne?

_____

B. *Talk about your answers with another student. Are they the same? Then check your answers with your teacher.*

Focus on Vocabulary

A. *Do you know the meanings of these words? Read each word aloud. Then put a ✓ (you know), ? (you aren't sure), or X (you don't know).*

_____ compete	_____ train	_____ record
_____ decide	_____ mistake	_____ adult
_____ distance	_____ miss	_____ moment
_____ weak		

B. *Read the passage to the end.*

Marathon Winner: Paula Radcliffe

Paula Radcliffe was born in England in 1973. She began running when she was seven. Her father sometimes competed in races for fun. But Paula was always very serious about running. She began winning races when she was still very young. Her first big success came in 1992 when she won the World Cross Country Championships for Juniors.

5 This was a good start to her career. But now Paula had to compete with adults. For a while, she didn't do very well. She also hurt her foot. In 1995 she won 5th place at the World Championships. In 1996 she won 5th place in the Olympics. During these years, Paula trained for many hours every day. But running wasn't the only thing in her life. Paula also finished high school and

10 university.

Then, in 2000 and 2001, she won the World Cross Country Championships. These were middle-distance races—5,000 or 10,000 meters. In 2002 she finally decided to run in a long-distance race, the Chicago

15 Marathon (26 miles/42 km). This was a big moment in her career. She not only won the race, she also broke the world record for women. The year 2000 was also important for another reason: Paula married her trainer, Gary Lough.

Over the next five years, she ran in eight marathons and won seven of

20 them. She also broke several other British and world records. Then Paula and Gary decided to have a child. She continued to train until a short time before the baby was born in January 2007. And she started training again soon after. She didn't want to miss the New York City Marathon in November 2007.

25 Many people said it was a mistake to run in the race. They thought she was too weak. Paula showed that they were wrong. It was a close race, but she won. She showed that she was the fastest woman long distance racer. And she showed that women can continue to compete after they have children.

C. Look back at the passage and circle the words from the list in part A. *(Some words may be in a different form: train → trained, adult → adults.)* Then underline all of the words you don't know.

D. Look up the underlined words in the dictionary and write them in your vocabulary notebook. *(See Part 2, Unit 1, page 71.)*

E. Check your understanding of the passage. Read it again if you need to. Write **T** *(true)* or **F** *(false)* before each sentence.

_____ 1. Paula always liked running.

_____ 2. Paula never finished school.

_____ 3. At first Paula ran middle-distance races.

_____ 4. Paula won a marathon the same year she had a baby.

F. Talk about your answers with another student. Are they the same? Then check all your work with your teacher.

EXERCISE 14

A. Read each sentence and circle the best meaning for the underlined word(s).

1. Her father sometimes <u>competed</u> in races for fun.
   a. practiced   b. looked   c. ran

2. But now Paula had to compete with <u>adults</u>.
   a. older people   b. children   c. teenagers

3. During these years, Paula <u>trained</u> for many hours every day.
   a. ran   b. studied   c. worked

4. These were middle-<u>distance</u> races—5,000 or 10,000 meters.
   a. difficulty   b. length   c. time

5. In 2002 she finally <u>decided</u> to run in a long-distance race, the Chicago Marathon (26 miles/42 km).
   a. told her father   b. thought it was best   c. didn't want

6. This was a big <u>moment</u> in her career.
   a. afternoon   b. long time   c. point in time

7. She not only won the race; she also broke the world <u>record</u> for women.
   a. best time   b. hit song   c. number of miles

8. She didn't want to <u>miss</u> the New York City Marathon in November, 2007.
   a. wait for   b. not be in   c. compete in

9. Many people said it was a <u>mistake</u> to run in the race.
   a. wrong thing to do   b. easy thing to do   c. expensive thing to do

10. They thought she was <u>too weak</u>.
    a. too fat   b. very unhappy   c. not strong

B. *Talk about your answers with another student. Are they the same?*

EXERCISE 15

A. *Complete the sentences with the words from the box. Use each word only once. Change the word for the sentence if necessary (plural, past tense, etc.).*

compete	train	decide	record	mistake
adult	distance	moment	miss	weak

1. It was a _____ to leave at eight o'clock this morning. There was a lot of traffic.

2. Carlos _____ the bus yesterday because he woke up late.

3. The bus tickets are $10 for _____ and $8 for children.

4. Maria _____ not to buy the car; it cost too much.

5. Mika broke the school _____ for the high jump.

6. After her long tennis game, she felt very _____.

7. Her house was just a short _____ from the school.

8. Thousands of runners _____ in the marathon.

9. Before a marathon, you have to _____ for many months.

10. He loved her from the _____ he saw her.

B. *Talk about your answers with another student. Are they the same?*

A. Write a sentence for each of the words in the box. Look at the sentences in Exercises 14 and 15 if you need help.

compete	train	decide	record	mistake
adult	distance	moment	miss	weak

1. _____
2. _____
3. _____
4. _____
5. _____
6. _____
7. _____
8. _____
9. _____
10. _____

B. Check your work with your teacher.

EXERCISE 17

A. Write the other parts of speech for each word. More than one answer is possible.

1. **train** (v)   noun: _____

2. **distance** (n)   adjective: _____
                      adverb: _____

3. **compete** (v)   noun: _____
                      adjective: _____
                      adverb: _____

4. decide (v) noun: _____

adjective: _____

adverb: _____

5. weak (adj) noun: _____

verb: _____

adverb: _____

B. *Talk about your answers with another student. Are they the same? Then check your answers with your teacher.*

C. *Write all the new words from Exercises 13–17 in your vocabulary notebook. Then make study cards. Study them alone and then with another student.*

Focusing on the Topic

What Is a Topic?

- A topic is something people talk or write about.
- It can be a thing, a person, or an idea.

The topic is important in written English. Writers think about the topic when they are writing. To understand their ideas, you need to look for the topic.

In this unit, you will practice thinking about the topic with lists of words. The topic of each list is a general word. It tells about the other words in the list.

Kinds of Topics

- The topic can be the name of a group of things or people.

  Example: Topic: _____*color*_____

  red   yellow   blue   white   black

  Explanation:
  All the words are names of colors.

- The topic can also be the name of a thing with many parts.

  Example: Topic: _____*computer*_____

  monitor   keyboard   hard drive   mouse   USB port

  Explanation:
  All the words are parts of a computer.

> **Note:** You do not need to know all the words in each group. You just need to find the topic. Try to find the topic without using a dictionary.

Finding the Topic

EXAMPLE

Find the topic in each list. Circle it and write it on the line.

pop   (music)   rock   country   classical   jazz

Topic: _____music_____

EXERCISE 1

A. Find the topic in each list. Circle it and write it on the line.

1. husband   cousin   wife   son   family   daughter
   Topic: _____

2. head   nose   mouth   ear   hair   eye
   Topic: _____

3. cat   dog   horse   pig   cow   animal
   Topic: _____

4. shirts   dresses   clothes   pants   coats   socks
   Topic: _____

5. afternoon   noon   midnight   evening   day   morning
   Topic: _____

6. walk   talk   sleep   live   smile   verb
   Topic: _____

7. apple   banana   orange   fruit   mango   pear
   Topic: _____

8. cake   dessert   ice cream   cookie   pie   fruit
   Topic: _____

9. vegetable   carrot   bean   lettuce   tomato   celery
   Topic: _____

10. table   stove   sink   chair   kitchen   refrigerator
    Topic: _____

B. Talk about your answers with another student. Are they the same?

C. Look up the new words in the dictionary and write them in your vocabulary notebook. *(See Part 2, Unit 1, page 71.)*

EXERCISE 2

A. Find the topic in each list. Circle it and write it on the line.

1. hotel   hospital   bank   school   building   house

   Topic: _____

2. breakfast   meal   dinner   lunch   snack   supper

   Topic: _____

3. arm   body   leg   back   head   foot

   Topic: _____

4. fork   spoon   cup   plate   knife   tableware

   Topic: _____

5. armchair   furniture   sofa   desk   bed   table

   Topic: _____

6. search   home   link   address   image   website

   Topic: _____

7. drink   soda   coffee   juice   water   beer

   Topic: _____

8. tree   flower   grass   garden   plant   bush

   Topic: _____

9. dollar   money   euro   yen   pound   franc

   Topic: _____

10. wheel   door   window   seat   engine   car

    Topic: _____

B. Talk about your answers with another student. Are they the same?

C. *Look up the new words in the dictionary and write them in your vocabulary notebook.*

EXERCISE 3

A. *Find a topic in the box for each list of words. Write it on the line.*

> people who work with money   people who work outside
> people who work with people   people who work with their hands
> ~~people who work in the government~~   people who work in a hospital
> people who often work at night   people who make music

1. mayor   president   governor   prime minister   senator
   Topic: *people who work in the government*

2. taxi driver   doctor   baker   police officer   telephone operator
   Topic: _____

3. doctor   orderly   nurse   technician   surgeon
   Topic: _____

4. violinist   pianist   conductor   soprano   drummer
   Topic: _____

5. artist   gardener   cook   surgeon   pianist
   Topic: _____

6. banker   cashier   accountant   trader   economist
   Topic: _____

7. gardener   football player   police officer   farmer   road worker
   Topic: _____

8. teacher   doctor   nurse   lawyer   psychologist
   Topic: _____

B. *Talk about your answers with another student. Are they the same?*

C. *Look up the new words in the dictionary and write them in your vocabulary notebook.*

Thinking of the Topic

The topic for each list should be just right for those words. It should not be too general (too big) or too specific (too small).

EXAMPLE
....

Think of a topic for the list and write it on the line.

> aunt   sister   mother   grandmother   daughter
>
> Topic: _girls and women in a family_

Explanation:
- This topic tells us that the words are all for people. And all the people are girls or women.
- The topic *family* is too general. A *family* also has men in it (for example: father, brother, son). But there are no men on the list.
- The topic *girls in a family* is too specific. Some of the people in the list are not young girls (for example: grandmother, mother, aunt).

Remember

The topic should be just right for the list of words—not too general and not too specific.

EXERCISE 4

A. *Read each list. Then write a topic. You may use a dictionary.*

1. chapter   page   paragraph   title   table of contents
   Topic: _____

2. skiing   sledding   speed skating   hockey   ice dancing
   Topic: _____

3. bedroom   kitchen   bathroom   hall   living room
   Topic: _____

4. bus   car   subway   plane   train

Topic: _____

5. pencil   pen   marker   chalk   crayon

Topic: _____

6. desk   computer   telephone   copy machine chair

Topic: _____

7. books   magazines newspapers messages blogs

Topic: _____

8. adjective noun   verb   pronoun   adverb

Topic: _____

9. chicken lamb   pork   beef   rabbit

Topic: _____

10. France   Spain   Finland   Ireland   Greece

Topic: _____

B. *Talk about your answers with another student. Are they the same? Then check your answers with your teacher.*

C. *Look up the new words in the dictionary. Write them in your vocabulary notebook with the parts of speech, the sentences, and the meanings.*

EXERCISE 5

A. *Read each list and write a topic. Then add one more word to the list.*

1. trees   bushes   path   bench   *flowers*

Topic: *park* _____

2. nine   fifteen   three   thirty   _____

Topic: _____

3. Seoul   Tokyo   Beijing   Hanoi   _____

Topic: _____

4. cake   balloons   candles   gifts   _____
   Topic: _____

5. ocean   river   lake   pond   _____
   Topic: _____

6. guitarist   drummer   pianist   singer   _____
   Topic: _____

7. banana   mango   pineapple   papaya   _____
   Topic: _____

8. cow   sheep   goat   pig   _____
   Topic: _____

9. California   Arizona   Colorado   Utah   _____
   Topic: _____

10. handlebar   pedal   seat   chain   _____
   Topic: _____

B. *Talk about your answers with another student. Are they the same? Then check your answers with your teacher.*

C. *Look up the new words in the dictionary. Write them in your vocabulary notebook with the parts of speech, the sentences, and the meanings.*

EXERCISE 6

A. *One word in each list doesn't belong to the topic. Cross out the word that doesn't belong. Then write the topic. You may use a dictionary.*

1. eighteen   ten   ~~eleven~~   twelve   seventy-two
   Topic: *even numbers* _____

2. lions   panthers   tigers   elephants   leopards
   Topic: _____

3. March   Tuesday   November   June   April
   Topic: _____

4. new   beautiful   clean   house   large

Topic: _____

5. carrot   hamburger   French fries   hot dog   fried chicken

Topic: _____

6. jump   run   jog   dance   sleep

Topic: _____

7. hour   city   month   day   week

Topic: _____

8. football   tennis   golf   skiing   basketball

Topic: _____

9. Egypt   South Africa   Mozambique   Zimbabwe   Rwanda

Topic: _____

10. gold   steel   silver   wood   iron

Topic: _____

B. *Talk about your answers with another student. Are they the same? Then check your answers with your teacher.*

C. *Look up the new words in the dictionary. Write them in your vocabulary notebook, with the parts of speech, the sentences, and the meanings.*

EXERCISE 7

A. *Think of five words for each topic and write them on a separate piece of paper. You may use a dictionary.*

- Kinds of weather
- Kinds of cars
- Parts of a skyscraper
- Places in a school
- Jobs that pay well
- Home electronics

B. *Talk about your answers with another student. Are they the same? Look up the new words in the dictionary. Then write them in your vocabulary notebook.*

Focus on Vocabulary

A. *Do you know the meanings of these words? Read each word aloud. Then put a ✓ (you know), ? (you aren't sure), or X (you don't know).*

_____ take care of	_____ rent	_____ notice
_____ camp	_____ headache	_____ cousin
_____ outside	_____ invite	_____ accident
_____ amount		

B. *Read the passage to the end.*

Marathon Winner: Robert Cheruiyot

Robert Cheruiyot is another famous marathon runner. He was born in Kenya in 1978. His parents were very poor. One day, his father left the family forever. After that, his mother could not take care of Robert and his brother.

For many years, Robert lived with his cousins. He worked for them, and
5   they paid for his school. It was a hard life, but he liked the school. Best of all, he liked the sports at school.

Then, one day, Robert's cousins didn't want him in their home anymore. They also didn't want to pay for Robert's school. Robert had to leave school, and he had no place to live. This was a difficult time for him. He found a job
10   so he could eat. But he didn't have enough money to rent a room. He had to sleep outside.

Finally, he found a place to live, and he started running. People soon noticed him because he was fast. He was invited to Moses Tanui's running
15   camp. Tanui was a famous marathon runner. Other people at the camp thought that Robert was eating too much and not running enough. But Tanui believed he had a future.

In 2001 Robert was invited to run in Italy. That was the beginning of his career. Soon he was winning races in Italy. In 2003 he decided to run in a big
20   race—the Boston Marathon. This was only his second long-distance race, but he won. He also broke the time record for Boston. With the prize money, he bought a farm in Kenya.

In 2006 he won again in Boston, and he won the Chicago Marathon. In
25   Chicago, he also had an accident. At the finish line, he fell and hit his head. He had to stay in the hospital for two days. For months after that, he had headaches.

30 But these headaches didn't slow him down. He won the Boston Marathon in 2007 and again in 2008. He also won the World Marathon Majors prize of $500,000. This was a huge amount of money for a boy who once had no shoes. But the important thing for him was that he now had a home. And now he could bring his family together again.

C. *Look back at the passage and circle the words on the list. (Some words may be in a different form: cousin → cousins.) Then underline all of the words you don't know.*

D. *Look up the underlined words in the dictionary. Write them in your vocabulary notebook with the parts of speech, the sentences, and the meanings.*

E. *Check your understanding of the passage. Read it again if you need to. Write T (true) or F (false) before each sentence.*

_____ 1. Robert had a happy family life.

_____ 2. Robert didn't want to go to school.

_____ 3. Moses Tanui helped Robert.

_____ 4. After his accident, he didn't win any more races.

F. *Talk about your answers with another student. Are they the same? Then check all your work with your teacher.*

EXERCISE 9

A. *Read each sentence and circle the best meaning for the underlined word(s).*

1. After that, his mother could not take care of Robert and his brother.
   a. look for   b. do things for   c. cry for

2. For many years, Robert lived with his cousins.
   a. relatives   b. friends   c. teachers

3. But he didn't have enough money to rent a room.
   a. put a table and   b. pay money to   c. buy
      chairs in   live in

4. He had to sleep outside.
   a. in a large building   b. in a hotel   c. not in a building

(continued)

5. People soon <u>noticed</u> him because he was fast.
   a. saw   b. liked   c. stopped

6. He was <u>invited</u> to Moses Tanui's running camp.
   a. dressed to go   b. asked to go   c. paid to go

7. He was invited to Moses Tanui's running <u>camp</u>.
   a. place for people   b. kind of race   c. village in
      to stay   the mountains

8. In Chicago he also <u>had an accident</u>.
   a. met some people   b. made some money   c. was hurt

9. He had to stay in the hospital for two days, and for months, <u>he had headaches</u>.
   a. he couldn't see   b. his head hurt   c. he wore a hat

10. This was <u>a huge amount of</u> money for a boy who once had no shoes.
   a. a little   b. not enough   c. a lot of

B. **Talk about your answers with another student. Are they the same?**

EXERCISE 10

A. **Complete the sentences with the words from the box. Use each word only once. Change the word for the sentence if necessary (plural, past tense, etc.).**

| take care of | rent | notice | camp | headache |
| cousin | outside | invite | accident | amount |

1. You should cook the vegetables in a small _____ of water.
2. In July we _____ a little house in the mountains.
3. The dog sleeps _____ in the summer.
4. His son had a bad car _____ last year.
5. Everyone _____ the new student because he was very tall.
6. Loud noises can give you a _____.
7. She went to a music _____ in the summer.
8. They _____ all their friends to a big party.
9. In the summer, I often visited my _____.
10. He _____ his grandmother when she was ill.

B. **Talk about your answers with another student. Are they the same?**

A. Write a sentence for each word in the box. Look at the sentences in Exercises 9 and 10 if you need help.

take care of	rent	notice	camp	headache
cousin	outside	invite	accident	amount

1. _____
2. _____
3. _____
4. _____
5. _____
6. _____
7. _____
8. _____
9. _____
10. _____

B. Check your work with your teacher.

EXERCISE 12

A. Write the other parts of speech. More than one answer is possible.

1. **accident** (n)   adjective: _____
                        adverb: _____

2. **invite** (v)   noun: _____
                      adjective: _____

3. **notice** (v)   noun: _____
                      adjective _____
                      adverb: _____

B. Talk about your answers with another student. Are they the same? Then check your answers with your teacher.

C. Write all of the new words from Exercises 8–12 in your vocabulary notebook. Then make study cards. Study them alone and then with another student.

Understanding Paragraphs

What Is a Paragraph?

A paragraph is a group of sentences about one topic. There is usually a sentence near the beginning of a paragraph that tells you the topic. All of the other sentences are also about the topic.

EXAMPLE

Read these passages. Are they paragraphs? Check (✓) your answer.

1. Every morning Susan Powers has a big breakfast. She drinks a glass of orange juice and a big cup of tea. She cooks two eggs and eats them with toast. She also eats some fruit—a banana or an apple. Susan says that she is ready to go to work after this breakfast.

   Paragraph __✓__   Not a paragraph _____

2. Every morning Susan Powers eats a big breakfast. She works in a bank in New York. Many people come to the bank. Some people go shopping before work. Others go shopping on weekends. On rainy days, they all bring their umbrellas to work.

   Paragraph _____   Not a paragraph __✓__

Explanation:
- Number 1 is a paragraph. All the sentences are about one topic: Susan's breakfast.
- Number 2 is not a paragraph. It's just a group of sentences about many different topics.

Remember

A paragraph has one topic. All the sentences are about that topic.

A. *Read these passages. Are they paragraphs? Check (✓) your answer.*

Paris

1.   Many visitors in Paris go to see the church of Nôtre Dame. It is often full of people. You can take a boat up and down the River Seine. The Seine is an important river in France. Another important river is the Rhône. It is in the south of France. The weather in the south of France is warm even in winter. French people like to go skiing in the Alps.

Paragraph _____   Not a paragraph _____

2.   Visitors come to Paris from all over the world. They visit museums and churches. They walk along the River Seine and the old streets. They go shopping in special small shops, in big stores, or at the outdoor markets. In the evening, they go to concerts or to the theater. And of course, they go to the many good restaurants.

Paragraph _____   Not a paragraph _____

3.   Paris is a very old city with many beautiful old buildings. One famous old building is the church of Nôtre Dame. Every visitor in Paris wants to see this church. Another old church is the Sainte Chapelle. It has very beautiful colored glass windows. In Paris, some beautiful old buildings were the homes of rich people. The most famous is the Louvre. It was the home of the King of France.

Paragraph _____   Not a paragraph _____

4.   Paris is home to more than two million people. About seven million people live close to Paris. London has more than seven million people. You can get anywhere in London with the Underground trains. The best way to get around Europe is by train. Travel by train does not make the air dirty. Air pollution is a big problem in many European cities.

Paragraph _____   Not a paragraph _____

B. *Talk about your answers with another student. Are they the same?*

A. *Read these passages. Are they paragraphs? Check (✓) your answer.*

Music

1.　　Music can help people in many ways. It can help people who are sick. When they listen to music, they forget they are sick. It can also help people who are unhappy. It makes them feel better about their lives. Music is like medicine for many people. But it is better than medicine in important ways. First, it is free. Second, it isn't bad for your body in any way.

　　Paragraph _____　　　Not a paragraph _____

2.　　Young people often like very loud music. They go to very loud concerts. They have loud music in their cars and in their rooms. And they listen to loud music on their mp3 players. All this loud music is bad for their ears. In fact, many young people already can't hear very well. When they are older, they may have serious problems with their hearing.

　　Paragraph _____　　　Not a paragraph _____

3.　　The piano is not difficult to play. But it is difficult to play well. Maurizio Pollini is a world-famous piano player. He is from Milan, Italy. Milan is a big city in the north of Italy. Lots of people from other countries visit Italy. They like Italian cheese and wine. Italian people eat lots of pasta. The first pizza was made in Naples, Italy.

　　Paragraph _____　　　Not a paragraph _____

4.　　Jazz music began in America. Many famous rock stars are English. In Boston you can go to good classical music concerts. John Williams writes music for the movies. Music can be a very important part of a movie. Bjork is a famous pop singer from Iceland. Irish music is popular in Ireland and in America. Chicago and St. Louis are both famous for blues music.

　　Paragraph _____　　　Not a paragraph _____

B. *Talk about your answers with another student. Are they the same?*

Choosing the Topic of a Paragraph

The topic tells what a paragraph is about. It should not be too general (too big) or too specific (too small).

Read the paragraph and circle the best topic.

Many water sports are popular at the seaside. The most popular water sport is swimming. Almost everyone likes being in the water. Some people also like swimming underwater and looking at fish. Another water sport is surfing. It is popular at beaches with big waves. Finally, sailing is very popular. Some people go out in small sailboats for a few hours. Others go out in larger boats for many days.

a. sports
(b.) water sports
c. sailing

Explanation:
- The answer is *b. water sports*. All of the sentences are about water sports.
- *Sports* is too general. This paragraph isn't about all kinds of sports, only water sports.
- *Sailing* is too specific. Not all of the sentences are about sailing.

EXERCISE 3

A. Read each paragraph and circle the best topic.

Triathlon Sports

1. *Triathlon* means "three sports." A triathlon is a race with three parts. Each part is a different sport. In a triathlon, first, you have to swim. Then you ride a bicycle many miles. And finally, you have to run for a long distance. The first triathlon was in Hawaii in 1978. There were 15 men in the race. They had to swim 2.4 miles (3.86 km), ride a bicycle for 112 miles (180 km), and run 26.2 miles (42 km). This race is now called the Ironman Triathlon. Today, there are triathlon races in many different countries.

    a. triathlon races
    b. swimming in a triathlon
    c. sports races today

2. The men and women who do triathlons are called *triathletes*. Triathletes must train hard all year to get ready. Every day they run, swim, and ride their bicycles for a long time. They must also do special exercises for their bodies. After many months of work, they are ready for a race. The very best triathletes try to win the race. The other people just try to finish. In fact, many people who start a triathlon are not able to finish.

   a. athletes
   b. exercises
   c. triathletes

3. Christine Wellington and Chris McCormack are both triathletes. Christine is from England, and Chris is from Australia. They were the winners of the 2007 Ironman Triathlon in Hawaii. Christine and Chris are both full-time athletes. All year they work on swimming, bicycling, and running. They get money for the races that they win. But they can only be in a few races every year. They will get hurt if they race too often. They also get money from companies that make sports clothes and shoes.

   a. winners of triathlons
   b. two triathletes
   c. the Ironman Triathlon

B. *Talk about your answers with another student. Are they the same?*

EXERCISE 4

A. *Read each paragraph and circle the best topic.*

Chocolate

1. Chocolate first came from Central America. Thousands of years ago, people there grew cocoa trees. They made a chocolate drink from the cocoa. It was very strong and not sweet at all. Then, in the 1600s, people in Spain began to make sweet chocolate drinks. Soon sweet chocolate drinks were popular in other countries. People also put chocolate in cakes and cookies. The first chocolate candy was made in England in 1849.

   a. chocolate
   b. chocolate drinks
   c. the history of chocolate

2. Today the cocoa for chocolate comes mostly from Africa and South America. The cocoa farmers in these countries often have small farms. They get very little money for their cocoa, and they are very poor. Some international groups are trying to help the farmers. They buy cocoa from the farmers at higher prices. Then they make chocolate and sell it as "fair trade" chocolate in the United States and Europe. It costs a little more than other chocolate, but it helps the farmers.

a. the cocoa farmers
b. chocolate today
c. farmers in Africa

3. Doctors say that too much chocolate is not good for you. Chocolate is made with sugar and fat. Sugar and fat are bad for your body in many ways. But a little dark chocolate is not bad for you. In fact, it is good for your blood and your heart. It also makes you feel happier and more awake. So when you are tired or sad, you should eat a little dark chocolate.

a. chocolate and your health
b. sugar and fat in chocolate
c. dark chocolate

B. *Talk about your answers with another student. Are they the same?*

Writing the Topic of a Paragraph

When you write the topic of a paragraph, it must be right for the paragraph.

EXAMPLE
....

Read the paragraph and write the topic.

In most parts of El Salvador, the weather is hot, and there is no change from summer to winter. In the mountains, it is a little cooler all year round. El Salvador sometimes has problems because of very bad weather. Hurricanes can bring terrible wind and rain. For example, Hurricane Mitch in 1998 killed hundreds of people. At other times, it doesn't rain enough. In 2001, there was very little rain, and people died because they didn't have enough food.

Topic: *the weather in El Salvador*

Explanation
- *The weather in El Salvador* is a good topic because it tells what the paragraph is about.
- The topic *El Salvador* is too general. A paragraph with this topic can be about lots of other things (for example: the people, the history, the food, etc.).
- The topic *hurricanes in El Salvador* is too specific. The paragraph doesn't talk only about hurricanes. It also talks about other kinds of weather.

Remember

A paragraph has one topic. All the sentences are about that topic.

EXERCISE 5

A. Read each paragraph and write the topic.

Central America

1. Central America is not large. It is much smaller than South America or North America. It is only about 420,000 square miles (700,000 square km). That is about the size of Texas. But Central America has many different kinds of land. There are tall mountains made by volcanoes. There are large lakes, small lakes, and many rivers. There are dry places with few plants and very wet places with lots of plants. There is a lot of coastline, where the land meets the sea. And there are many islands.

   Topic: _____

2. For scientists, Central America is a good place to study many kinds of animals. Central America is like a bridge between North and South America. Long ago, animals moved into Central America from the north and the south. They found good places to live, and they stayed there. Today all these animals live together. Other animals live in Central America only for part of the year. Some birds and butterflies, for example, live in North America in the summer and in Central America in the winter.

   Topic: _____

3.   The first people arrived in Central America about 18,000 years ago. They found lots of food and good places to live. Over the years, the number of people grew. By 1492, there were about 7,680,000 people living in Central America. They spoke 62 different languages. Some lived in small villages. Others, like the Maya, lived in cities. Then the Europeans arrived. In a very few years, 90 percent of the people in Central America died. Some were killed by the Europeans, and others died from diseases.

Topic: _____

B. *Talk about your answers with another student. Are they the same? Then check your answers with your teacher.*

EXERCISE 6

A. *Read each paragraph and write the topic.*

Diamonds

1.   It is not easy to get diamonds. There are diamonds in Africa, Australia, Russia, and Canada. In most of these places, they are deep underground. People have to dig far down to get them. In South Africa, for example, diamonds are sometimes found more than 3,000 feet (1,000 meters) underground. In other places, diamonds are on the ground or in rivers. But they are hard to find. Very few people find big diamonds and become rich.

Topic: _____

2.   Why are diamonds so expensive? First of all, they are very beautiful. In the past, kings and queens wanted to wear diamonds. Today famous people like to wear them. A diamond on your finger shows that you are successful and rich. Diamonds also have other meanings. In the United States and in India, for example, they mean love. They are something special that you give to someone special. Finally, diamonds are very useful because they are very hard. People can use them to cut metal and other stones.

Topic: _____

(continued)

3.   The high price of diamonds means that people do terrible things to get them. People fight wars and kill each other over diamonds. This happened in the past in India. These days it is still happening in Africa. The civil wars in Sierra Leone and the Congo happened partly because of diamonds. In those wars, both sides got money from diamonds. They used the money to buy guns, pay soldiers, and keep fighting. Because of diamond money, many people lost their homes and died.

Topic: _____

B. *Talk about your answers with another student. Are they the same? Then check your answers with your teacher.*

EXERCISE 7

A. *Read each paragraph and write the topic.*

Hot Spots

1.   Hot spots are special areas on the earth that scientists are studying. They are special because they are full of many kinds of plants and animals. Some of the plants and animals don't live anywhere else. These areas are changing fast. People are cutting down forests. They are making farms, building roads, factories, and towns. There is less and less land for the plants and animals. The scientists are worried about these areas. Every year, there are fewer kinds of plants and animals. Some of them are in danger. Soon they may become extinct. That means they will be gone forever from the earth.

Topic: _____

2.   One hot spot is the Philippines. This area includes more than 7,100 islands. In the past, there were forests on all the islands. These forests had over 6,000 kinds of plants. They also had many kinds of birds and other animals. Then, in the 1980s and 1990s, the number of people in the Philippines grew fast. The forests soon began to disappear. Some people cut down trees to sell the wood. Other people burned trees to make space for farms. Today, there are very few forests left. Because of this, many of the forest plants and animals are in danger.

Topic: _____

3.   Scientists are worried. Many kinds of plants and animals will soon be extinct. The last time many plants and animals became extinct was at the time of the dinosaurs. That was millions of years ago. We don't know why the dinosaurs became extinct. We do know that there were big changes at that time. The earth changed, the weather changed, and the dinosaurs all died. Scientists say that the earth is changing today. The land is also changing, and the weather is changing. But this time, people are making the changes. And this time, the changes are happening much faster.

Topic: _____

B.   *Talk about your answers with another student. Are they the same? Then check your answers with your teacher.*

EXERCISE 8

A.   *Complete each paragraph. Write the letter of the correct sentence from the box. Then write the topic.*

> a. It was about the problems between white people and black people in Rhodesia.
> b. Her words help us understand the way African Americans speak and think.
> c. He writes books about different places, so he has to go to those places.

Writers

1.   Thomas Keneally is an Australian writer. He lives in Sydney with his family, but he is often away from home. _____. One of his books is about the American Civil War, and another is about Ireland in the 19th century. His most famous book is about Nazi Germany during World War II. It tells the story of more than 1,000 Jewish people and a man named Oskar Schindler. Schindler helped these people live through those terrible times. The book, *Schindler's List*, was made into a movie.

Topic: _____

(continued)

2.   Doris Lessing is a British writer, but she grew up in Rhodesia (now Zimbabwe, Africa). She left school when she was 13 and started working at 15. She wrote her first book, *The Grass is Singing* in 1949. _____. In 1962, she wrote her most famous book, *The Golden Notebook*. In her later life, Lessing wrote science fiction books about the future. In 2007, she won the Nobel Prize for Literature. She was the ninth woman to get the prize. At 86 years old, she was the oldest writer to win.

Topic: _____

3.   Toni Morrison is an African-American writer. She often writes about African-American women. Her books tell about their lives and about the terrible things that happen to these women. We see the stories through their eyes, and we learn what they are thinking and feeling. In Morrison's books, the language is very different. She uses words in a way that is special. _____. In 1993, Morrison won the Nobel Prize for Literature. Two of her most famous books are *Beloved* and *Jazz*.

Topic: _____

B. **Talk about your answers with another student. Are they the same? Then check your answers with your teacher.**

EXERCISE 9

A. **The sentences in the box on page 193 are from paragraphs about two topics:**

1. Drinks that are very good for you
2. Drinks that are not good for you

Write the number of the topic after each sentence.

Milk is another healthy drink. _____

Drinking too much can keep you awake at night. _____

Many people drink Coca-Cola,® but it is not good for you. _____

It is very good for children because it builds strong bones. _____

A little coffee is okay, but lots of coffee is not good. _____

Orange juice is one of these healthy drinks. _____

Some doctors think this is the way to a healthy life. _____

It has lots of sugar, so it is bad for your teeth. _____

So drink lots of orange juice and milk. _____

Another drink that can be bad for you is coffee. _____

B. **Now complete the paragraphs with sentences from part A. Put the sentences in logical order. (More than one order is possible.)**

Drinks that Are Very Good for You

1. Some kinds of drinks are very good for your health. _____

_____

_____

_____

_____

_____

_____

_____

Drinks that Are Not Good for You

2. Some popular drinks are not good for your health. _____

_____

_____

_____

_____

_____

_____

C. **Talk about your answers with another student. Are they the same? Then check your work with your teacher.**

A. *One sentence in each paragraph does not belong to the topic. Find the sentence and cross it out. Then write the topic of the paragraph.*

Green Homes

1.   Do you want a green home? A green home is better for the Earth. It puts fewer chemicals into the air and the water. It is also better for you. ~~The price of houses is going up year after year.~~ You will feel better, and you will save money in a green home. It is not difficult to make your home more green. First, you have to study your home and think about how you do things. Then you will have to make some changes. Many of these changes are easy to make.

Topic: _____

2.   You can make your home greener by using less electricity. Most electricity comes from burning coal or oil. That makes the air very dirty. So you should turn off the lights when you leave a room. And you should use low-energy light bulbs. Thomas Edison made the first light bulb. These light bulbs give a lot of light, but they don't use much electricity. You should also turn off the television and computer when you are not using them. Do not leave them on standby because that uses electricity, too.

Topic: _____

3.   A green home also looks green because it has lots of plants in it. Plants are nice to look at. Many plants grow better in the sun. They are also good for you because they help make the air cleaner. First, all plants put oxygen in the air. This is good because people need oxygen. Some plants can also take bad chemicals out of the air. These chemicals can come from many things in a house—furniture, rugs, paint, or detergent. Plants that clean the air are not difficult to take care of and you can find them anywhere.

Topic: _____

B. *Talk about your answers with another student. Are they the same?*

A. *Choose a topic from the box. Write a paragraph with five or six sentences. Remember, all the sentences should be about the topic.*

> a special person in my life   my favorite teacher
> a nice place to visit   my favorite book/movie

_____

_____

_____

_____

_____

_____

_____

_____

_____

B. *Show your paragraph to another student. Ask:* **Is this a good paragraph? Why or why not?**

Focus on Vocabulary

A. *Do you know the meaning of the words on the list below? Read each word aloud. Then put a* ✓ *(you know),* ? *(you aren't sure), or* X *(you don't know).*

_____ peace	_____ actress	_____ really
_____ director	_____ dream	_____ energy
_____ grow up	_____ able to	_____ recognize
_____ partner		

B. *Read the passage to the end.*

Salma Hayek

    Salma Hayek was born in Mexico in 1966. Her father was a Lebanese businessman, and her mother was a Mexican opera singer. The name *Salma* means peace in Arabic, but Salma was not a peaceful child. She was full of energy. She loved to be in the middle of a group of people. When she saw her
5   first movie, she made a decision. She wanted to be an actress when she grew up.

    Salma was a difficult teenager. Her parents sent her to several schools, but she was not happy, or the schools were not happy with her. They even sent her to a school in the United States. But she got into trouble too often, and they
10   sent her home again.

    She began university in Mexico City, but she was not really interested in studying. She just wanted to act. First, she acted at the university theater. Then, when she was only 22, she got a part in a popular television program called "Teresa." That show made her famous in Mexico.

15   But for Salma, it wasn't enough to be famous in Mexico. She wanted to be famous in Hollywood. In 1991, she went to Los Angeles and began to look for parts in the movies there. She was beautiful, and she was a good actress. But for several years, she wasn't able to get any big parts. It wasn't easy for a Mexican to become a star in Hollywood.

20   Finally, a director named Robert Rodriguez noticed her. She starred in his film, *Desperado*. After that, she got some other serious parts in movies. She worked with stars like George Clooney and Russell Crowe. Finally, she was a famous actress, and she was recognized everywhere.

But her dream was to make a movie about Frida Kahlo, the famous
25 Mexican painter. This dream came true in 2002. This movie was a big success
and won many prizes.

In 2007, at the age of 41, Salma became a mother. She and her partner,
Francois-Henri Pinault had a daughter, Valentina.

C. *Look back at the passage and circle the words on the list. (Some words may
be in a different form: grow up → grew up.) Then underline all of the words
you don't know.*

D. *Look up the underlined words in the dictionary and write them in your
vocabulary notebook. (See Part 2, Unit 1, page 71.)*

E. *Check your understanding of the passage. Read it again if you need to. Write
T (true) or F (false) before each sentence.*

_____ 1. When she was a child, Salma wanted to be an actress.

_____ 2. She was a good student.

_____ 3. She was not well known in Mexico.

_____ 4. Her movie about Frida Kahlo was not successful.

F. *Talk about your answers with another student. Are they the same? Then
check all your work with your teacher.*

EXERCISE 13

A. *Read each sentence and circle the best meaning for the underlined word(s).*

1. The name *Salma* means <u>peace</u> in Arabic, but Salma was not a
peaceful child.
   a. quiet   b. sadness   c. happiness

2. She was <u>full of energy</u>.
   a. sometimes angry   b. often crying   c. always moving

3. She wanted to be <u>an actress</u> when she grew up.
   a. in a big house   b. in the movies   c. a singer

4. She wanted to be an actress when she <u>grew up</u>.
   a. was a mother   b. was an adult   c. was in school

(continued)

5. She began university in Mexico City, but she was not <u>really</u> interested in studying.
   a. in fact   b. sometimes   c. maybe

6. But for several years, she <u>wasn't able</u> to get any big parts.
   a. didn't want to   b. didn't try to   c. couldn't

7. Finally, a <u>director</u> named Robert Rodriguez noticed her.
   a. person who makes movies   b. person who acts in movies   c. person who watches movies

8. Finally, she was a famous actress, and she was <u>recognized</u> everywhere
   a. studied   b. known   c. followed

9. But her <u>dream</u> was to make a movie about Frida Kahlo, the famous Mexican painter.
   a. hope   b. fear   c. business

10. She and her <u>partner</u>, Francois-Henri Pinault, had a daughter, Valentina.
    a. person she knows   b. person she grew up with   c. person she lives with

B. **Talk about your answers with another student. Are they the same?**

EXERCISE 14

A. **Complete the sentences with the words from the box. Use each word only once. Change the word for the sentence if necessary (plural, past tense, etc.).**

peace	actress	really	director	dream
energy	grow up	able to	recognize	partner

1. The teacher _____ didn't know what to do about Suki.
2. When she was ill, she didn't have much _____.
3. My _____ is to be a writer some day.
4. Nicole Kidman is a beautiful woman and she's a good
   _____.
5. He was born in Italy, but he _____ in America.
6. He moved to the countryside so he could live in _____.

7. I didn't _____ him with white hair.
8. The _____ of this movie is Polish.
9. James and his _____ decided that they wanted to get a dog.
10. Three days after the snowstorm, we were finally _____ leave.

B. *Talk about your answers with another student. Are they the same?*

EXERCISE 15

A. *Write a sentence for each word in the box. Look at the sentences in Exercises 13 and 14 if you need help.*

peace	actress	really	director	dream
energy	grow up	able to	recognize	partner

1. _____
2. _____
3. _____
4. _____
5. _____
6. _____
7. _____
8. _____
9. _____
10. _____

B. *Check your work with your teacher.*

EXERCISE 16

A. *Write the other parts of speech of each word. There is more than one possible answer.*

1. **able** (adj)   noun: _____

(continued)

2. actress (n)　　　noun (another form): _____

verb: _____

3. grow up (v)　　　noun: _____

adjective: _____

4. recognize (v)　　　noun: _____

adjective: _____

5. peace (n)　　　adjective: _____

adverb: _____

6. director (n)　　　noun (another form): _____

verb: _____

adjective: _____

adverb: _____

7. energy (n)　　　verb: _____

adjective: _____

adverb: _____

8. dream (n)　　　verb: _____

adjective: _____

adverb: _____

9. really (adv)　　　adjective: _____

noun: _____

verb: _____

B. *Talk about your answers with another student. Are they the same?
Then check your answers with your teacher.*

C. *Write all of the new words from Exercise 12–16 in your vocabulary notebook.
Then make study cards. Study them alone and then with another student.*

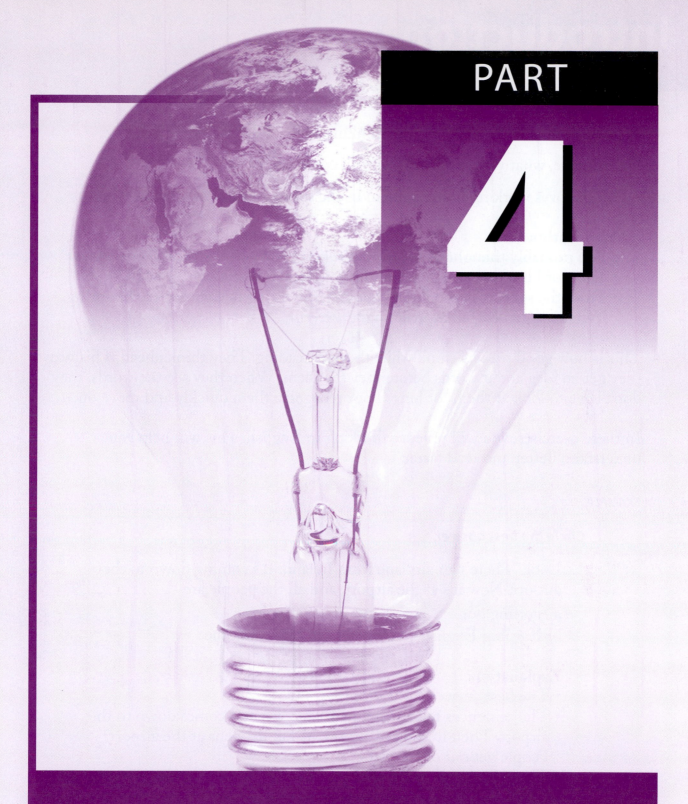

PART

4

Thinking in English

Introduction

When you read in English, are you thinking about what will come next?

For example, what word do you think will come next?

Linda loves working in her garden. In the spring, it's full of _____.

Explanation:
- You probably thought of the word *flowers*.
- The word is a noun—only a noun can follow "full of."
- From the sentences you know that it is something in a garden in the spring. What is a garden full of in spring? *Flowers*.

This is how good readers think while they are reading. They think ahead. This way they get an idea about words before they see them. When they see the words, they don't have to look at them for long. They recognize them quickly and move on.

In these exercises, you will practice thinking in English. This will help you understand better and read faster.

EXAMPLE

Circle the best answer.

1. Look! There's an airplane from Ireland. It's coming down to the airport. Now it's at the airport, and all the people are _____.
   a. getting out
   b. learning English
   c. sleeping
   d. buying clothes

   Explanation:
   - The best answer is *a. getting out*.
   - The sentences tell about an airplane. First, it comes down to the airport. Then it is at the airport. What happens at the airport? People get out of the plane.
   - The other answers are about things that people do after they get out.

2. When we arrived at the house, there was a big dog in the yard. When he saw us, he looked angry. We ran away because we were _____ .

a. happy

c. sad

b. afraid

d. hungry

Explanation:
- The best answer is *b. afraid*.
- How do you feel when you see a big, angry dog? You feel afraid. You don't feel happy, sad, or hungry.

Guidelines for *Thinking in English* Exercises:

- Do some exercises every day.

- Do the exercises in order. The exercises in Unit 1 are the easiest. The exercises in Unit 3 are the most difficult.

- Try to guess the meaning of new words. Use a dictionary if you need the word for the answer.

- Think in English to find the correct answer.

- Work quickly. Remember, your first guess is often the right one!

EXERCISE 1

A. Circle the best answer.

1. Last night, Miriam had a party with her friends. They had lots of things to eat and drink. There was also good music. Everyone stayed until _____.

   a. early   c. late
   b. lunch   d. Tuesday

2. There are many kinds of apples. Some are green, some are yellow, and some are red. They are all good to _____.

   a. eat   c. feel
   b. drink   d. see

3. Could you please help me? Dinner is almost ready. Here are the forks, knives, and spoons. Please put them _____.

   a over the table   c. at the store
   b. on the table   d. in the kitchen

4. My friend has 15 cats. She has some gray cats and some brown cats. She has a beautiful, young white cat, but she has no _____.

   a. brown cats   c. brown dogs
   b. little cats   d. black cats

5. Juan never drinks tea in the morning. But he often drinks tea in the afternoon. He drinks tea and eats a piece of cake _____.

   a. for lunch   c. at 4:00 A.M.
   b. at 9:00 A.M.   d. for breakfast

6. Edwin is a cook in a small restaurant. He cooks lunch and dinner. He doesn't cook breakfast because the restaurant is closed _____.

   a. in the morning   c. in the evening
   b. at lunch time   d. on Tuesdays

B. Talk about your answers with another student. Are they the same?

A. *Circle the best answer.*

1. Sam Wood is a manager for a big company. He has a big desk and a big chair in a big office. But he is not a big man. He is very _____.
   a. tall
   b. old
   c. short
   d. large

2. My father reads the newspaper every evening. First, he reads about the world. Then he reads about our town. Finally, he reads the sports _____.
   a. pages
   b. games
   c. books
   d. football

3. There was a fire in our town yesterday. A house burned to the ground. But the family was not at home, so no people were _____.
   a. happy
   b. ill
   c. hurt
   d. dangerous

4. Surya is away in New York for some business meetings. She calls her office every day. Her manager wants to talk with _____.
   a. him
   b. her
   c. them
   d. me

5. In the spring, the grass and the trees are green. The flowers are pretty. It's a nice time of year to _____.
   a. visit gardens
   b. study English
   c. go shopping
   d. play music

6. Sandra is not happy about her job. Every day she has to meet with the manager. She doesn't like _____.
   a. meetings
   b. studying
   c. the food
   d. her clothes

B. *Talk about your answers with another student. Are they the same?*

A. Circle the best answer.

1. Manuela lives in the south of Spain. The weather is never very cold or wet there. It's warm and sunny _____.
   a. only in summer
   b. for a few months
   c. almost all year
   d. in Morocco

2. My father got a new clock last week. It's a very good clock. It's never fast or slow. It always has the _____.
   a. wrong time
   b. first time
   c. last time
   d. correct time

3. In Norway, winter days are short. The sun comes up late, and it goes down early. There are only a few hours of _____.
   a. nighttime
   b. daylight
   c. springtime
   d. weather

4. Chen has a new job in a computer store. A lot of people come to the store. He answers their questions, and he _____.
   a. gives them computers
   b. sells them computers
   c. buys them computers
   d. sells them books

5. Bus drivers are often very friendly. They have to drive the bus for many hours. They like to talk to the people _____.
   a. on the bus
   b. on the telephone
   c. in their cars
   d. in restaurants

6. When you have to cross a street, you must remember to look both ways. Look to the right and look _____.
   a. up and down
   b. at the people
   c. for a policeman
   d. to the left

B. Talk about your answers with another student. Are they the same?

A. Circle the best answer.

1. A big black cat lives in that house. It sits in the window all day. It likes to look at the people _____.
   a. in the house
   b. on television
   c. on the street
   d. in boats

2. Today young American women don't wear skirts very often. Most of the time they wear _____.
   a. hats
   b. coats
   c. shirts
   d. pants

3. Leo has a very old car. It's 20 years old! It's not very beautiful, and it's not very fast. But it always _____.
   a. goes
   b. stops
   c. comes
   d. breaks

4. On an airplane, you can't lie down. You can't put your feet up. There's always noise, and there's always light. It's not easy to _____.
   a. wake up
   b. take off
   c. get out
   d. fall asleep

5. These days you can do many jobs at home. You need a computer and a telephone to work at home. But you don't need a _____.
   a. able
   b. car
   c. job
   d. lunch

6. The *Call of the Wild* is a famous book by Jack London. It tells the story of a dog named Buck. This is a good book for people who love _____.
   a. animals
   b. movies
   c. science
   d. telephones

B. Talk about your answers with another student. Are they the same?

A. Circle the best answer.

1. Sometimes it's not easy to go to sleep at night. You start thinking about lots of things, and then you _____.
   a. can't stop
   b. go to sleep
   c. get in bed
   d. go to work

2. The first cell phone was made in 1972. It was very big and heavy. Cell phones today are very different. They're _____.
   a. very expensive
   b. also very heavy
   c. small and light
   d. made in Finland

3. The hotel room was very beautiful. It had big windows over the river. It had a big bed and a nice table. It also had a very large _____.
   a. dining room
   b. bathroom
   c. door
   d. telephone

4. Mara is getting a new pink dress. It's very pretty. Mara is very happy, but her mother is not. The dress is very _____.
   a. pretty
   b. old
   c. expensive
   d. long

5. Pilar is in bed. The doctor says she's very sick. She has to take some medicine. She shouldn't get out of bed. This week she won't be at _____.
   a. television
   b. home
   c. school
   d. time

6. Look at the back of my car! The light is broken. There's glass on the road. Who did that? I think another car hit _____.
   a. the door
   b. my car
   c. the road
   d. a wall

B. Talk about your answers with another student. Are they the same?

A. Circle the best answer.

1. Those shoes are very beautiful, but they're also very expensive. I can't buy them now. I don't have much _____.
   a. color   c. shoes
   b. money   d. work

2. Frank doesn't like to visit hospitals for children. He says they are sad places. It makes him sad to see so many sick boys and _____.
   a. girls   c. mothers
   b. doctors   d. medicines

3. Most schools now have computers. The children learn about them in their classes. The teachers use them for their _____.
   a. homes   c. books
   b. schools   d. lessons

4. Pedro didn't want to get out of bed. He didn't want to have breakfast or go to work. He wanted to _____.
   a. go home   c. sleep more
   b. take the bus   d. go to school

5. Susan and Sam don't eat French food very often. There's only one French restaurant in their town. The food there isn't very _____.
   a. old   c. open
   b. bad   d. good

6. Donna wants to be a doctor. She likes children, so she wants to be a children's doctor. Some day she wants to go to Africa and help African _____.
   a. animals   c. schools
   b. children   d. teachers

B. Talk about your answers with another student. Are they the same?

A. *Circle the best answer.*

1. Anna is a student at the University of Texas. This is her third year. She is studying Spanish. She wants to be a _____.

    a. French teacher   c. police officer
    b. children's doctor   d. Spanish teacher

2. Some birds don't like cold weather. They live in the north in the summer. Then, in the fall, they fly south to a _____.

    a. warmer place   c. colder place
    b. bigger place   d. smaller place

3. Ines always put her baby to bed after lunch. Sometimes the baby slept, but often he cried. He didn't want to stay in bed. He wanted to _____.

    a. get up   c. sleep
    b. eat   d. wake up

4. Soccer is a very popular sport. Men and boys play it all around the world. In many countries, women and girls also play _____.

    a. sports   c. soccer
    b. tennis   d. games

5. Do you write with your left hand or your right hand? Most people write with their right hand. Only about ten percent of people write with their _____.

    a. right hand   c. foot
    b. left hand   d. pencil

6. John came to work late again today. He is late almost every morning. What's the problem? Why is he always late? Doesn't he have a _____?

    a. clock   c. bedroom
    b. bus   d. computer

B. *Talk about your answers with another student. Are they the same?*

A. *Circle the best answer.*

1. Yuriko doesn't eat the school lunch. She says the food is terrible. She likes to bring a lunch from _____.
   a. school
   b. work
   c. home
   d. class

2. In some jobs, you have to stand up for many hours. For example, nurses and waiters are always _____.
   a. on the telephone
   b. in the room
   c. on a chair
   d. on their feet

3. Peter is 11 years old. He likes running and playing. He doesn't like reading because he doesn't want to _____.
   a. sit still
   b. go home
   c. talk to girls
   d. play tennis

4. Yesterday the lights went out in the evening. We couldn't watch television or use the computer. So we sat in the dark and _____.
   a. wrote e-mails
   b. talked with each other
   c. saw a movie
   d. played computer games

5. Peter is learning to play the piano. He plays it morning, afternoon, and evening. At first, he couldn't play very well. Now he can play _____.
   a. very often
   b. much worse
   c. very little
   d. much better

6. Why didn't you come to the party last night? We called you, but you didn't answer the phone. Did you have a problem with the _____?
   a. car
   b. computer
   c. book
   d. television

B. *Talk about your answers with another student. Are they the same?*

EXERCISE 1

A. *Circle the best answer.*

1. Monica had a very big suitcase. It was also heavy. But she could walk far with her suitcase because it had _____.
   a. books
   b. wheels
   c. pictures
   d. nothing

2. The Perez family likes to go to a Cuban restaurant. They go every Saturday evening. They meet friends at the restaurant, and they have a good _____.
   a. restaurant
   b. meal
   c family
   d. lunch

3. Raissa's favorite color is blue. She has lots of blue clothes, a blue car, and a blue house. But she doesn't have blue eyes! Her eyes are _____.
   a. big
   b. brown
   c. open
   d. blue

4. The city of Edinburgh, Scotland, is full of history. It has a beautiful castle, a beautiful church, and many other _____.
   a. new movie theaters
   b. good restaurants
   c. parks and gardens
   d. nice old buildings

5. Long airplane rides are not fun. You have to stay in your seat for a long time. You can't stand up for long, and you can't _____.
   a. sit down
   b. read books
   c. eat any food
   d. walk very far

6. Today many young people don't know how to cook. They buy food that is ready to eat, or they go to _____.
   a. restaurants
   b. the supermarket
   c. the movies
   d. work late

B. *Talk about your answers with another student. Are they the same?*

EXERCISE 2

A. *Circle the best answer.*

1. My cat knows when it's her dinner time. She stands in the kitchen and makes a lot of noise. Then I have to _____.
   a. go to the store
   b. give her food
   c. wait for her
   d. make coffee

2. You can't go in the building now. Something terrible happened. The police are talking to people and asking a lot of _____.
   a. questions
   b. ideas
   c. answers
   d. phone calls

3. Harold works for a computer company. It's a big company and it has offices around the world. He often has to go to other countries _____.
   a. for vacation
   b. to get home
   c. on the weekend
   d. for work

4. Last summer we went to the seaside. We stayed in a little red house. From the house, we could see the water. It was a great place. I hope we can stay _____.
   a. in another house
   b. home this year
   c. there again
   d. far away

5. Did you listen to the radio this morning? They said there was a terrible storm in Florida. Many people lost their homes, and two people _____.
   a. died
   b. went
   c. stayed
   d. lived

6. Some children are afraid of the dark. They don't like it because they can't see in the dark. At night, they always want the _____.
   a. lights on
   b. lights off
   c. door closed
   d. music on

B. *Talk about your answers with another student. Are they the same?*

A. Circle the best answer.

1. I like to go to the new store on Main Street. The people who work there are very friendly. They always smile and say hello. And they help you _____.
   a. find things   c. sell things
   b. build things   d. do things

2. There are many students from other countries at the university. Some of them know English well already. But many students don't _____.

   a. study languages   c. speak it well
   b. learn to speak   d. know Chinese

3. Why wasn't Juanita in class yesterday? Tanya says Juanita had an accident. Do you know what happened? I called Juanita's home, but _____.
   a. she was home   c. there was no answer
   b. Tanya doesn't know d. she has no phone

4. Many children don't like to eat vegetables. They like bread, pasta, meat, and sweet things. But they don't like _____.
   a. beans or peas   c. lunch or dinner
   b. spaghetti   d. cakes or cookies

5. Are you going to the store? Could you buy some more soap for the washing machine? There isn't any more, and I need to _____.
   a. wash some dishes   c. wash some clothes
   b. take a bath   d. buy some clothes

6. Many students went to the meeting yesterday evening. There were 50 students, but there were only about 40 chairs in the room. Some students had to _____.
   a. lie on beds   c. walk around
   b. sit on the floor   d. stand on chairs

B. Talk about your answers with another student. Are they the same?

A. Circle the best answer.

1. Dan is an English teacher in Japan. He works for a big Japanese company. Some people in the company need to speak English at work, so Dan teaches them _____.
   a. about the Japanese
   b. business English
   c. about business
   d. American history

2. Lorraine likes to have plants in her home, but she is not good with them. She gives them too much water or not enough water. In a short while, they _____.
   a. always die
   b. grow fast
   c. are beautiful
   d. fall down

3. If you need a break from work, go to a small island. It's a good place for a quiet vacation. There aren't many things to see. You can just sleep and do _____.
   a. exercises
   b. work
   c. everything
   d. nothing

4. Last weekend, some thieves got into the school. They took some computers and some video cameras. Now the school has to _____.
   a. sell old ones
   b. buy new rooms
   c. buy new ones
   d. sell new ones

5. For many months, it didn't rain. The land was very dry, and the rivers were empty. Farmers couldn't grow anything, and the price of food _____.
   a. went down
   b. went up
   c. didn't change
   d. was cheap

6. Tommy cries every morning because he doesn't want to go to school. He doesn't like the other children, and he doesn't like _____.
   a. his mother
   b. the street
   c. his teacher
   d. his breakfast

B. Talk about your answers with another student. Are they the same?

A. *Circle the best answer.*

1. Do you want to be a taxi driver? First, you have to pass a test. They will ask you questions about the car. They will also ask you questions about the _____.

   a. restaurants
   b. roads
   c. buses
   d. weather

2. Susanna is a teacher. She often has meetings. Sometimes she meets with the students and sometimes with the other teachers. She also has meetings with the _____.

   a. brothers and sisters
   b. pencils and paper
   c. men and women
   d. mothers and fathers

3. Ron Winston lives in Canada. He likes playing sports a lot. His favorite sports are winter sports. He loves skiing and ice skating. In fact, Ron loves the winter and _____.

   a. the summer
   b. cold weather
   c. traveling
   d. warm weather

4. Stella can't find her cell phone. It was in her room yesterday, but today it's not there. She thinks Luis took it, and now she's very _____.

   a. sick with a cold
   b. ready for class
   c. happy with her phone
   d. angry with Luis

5. Potatoes are usually very good to eat. But they're not good when they're green. If you find a green potato, you should not eat it. Green potatoes can make you _____.

   a. well
   b. better
   c. sick
   d. afraid

6. Rob is very busy. He doesn't have time to do sports or go to the gym. He wants to get exercise, so he never uses the elevator in his building. He lives on the 30th floor, so he has to climb _____.

   a. a lot of stairs
   b. a few stairs
   c. downstairs
   d. far away

B. *Talk about your answers with another student. Are they the same?*

A. *Circle the best answer.*

1. Shelley is a terrible student this year. She doesn't go to classes, and she doesn't do any homework. Her parents are _____.
   a. happy with her   c. not happy with her
   b. good students   d. terrible parents

2. Yesterday the children found a cat. It was very small and young, and it was all alone. The poor thing was very hungry, so they gave it _____.
   a. something to eat   c. lots of love
   b. a nice warm bed   d. a fun toy

3. Jin often doesn't have time to eat lunch at work. She only has time for coffee. When she comes home from work, she's very hungry. She usually _____.
   a. doesn't eat   c. reads a book
   b. has a snack   d. has no breakfast

4. Stephen King is a famous American writer. His books and stories are often best-sellers. Millions of people buy his books and _____.
   a. see movies   c. read them
   b. sell them   d. write them

5. Suki didn't know any other students at first, but now she knows many of them. After class, she often meets them in the café. She says they _____.
   a. are very friendly   c. never talk to her
   b. usually go home   d. read the newspaper

6. Every night a cat comes into Sam's yard. It cries and cries, and it wakes up Sam. He gets angry and goes out to the yard. But he can never _____.
   a. hear the cat   c. change the cat
   b. talk to the cat   d. find the cat

B. *Talk about your answers with another student. Are they the same?*

A. *Circle the best answer.*

1. There's a bridge over a river in Chicago. This bridge usually stays down, and cars go over it. Every hour it goes up so boats can go down the river. When the bridge is up, the cars _____.

   a. go down the river
   b. have to go over it
   c. have to wait
   d. can go faster

2. Last week my cat had a big fight with another cat. After that, she stayed away for three days. Then she came back home. Poor thing. She was _____.

   a. badly hurt
   b. very happy
   c. not alive
   d. a big cat

3. Do you like to listen to very loud music? This can be bad for your ears. You can hurt them with loud music, and then you won't _____.

   a. play well
   b. feel well
   c. see well
   d. hear well

4. Today was a beautiful day. It wasn't very hot, and it wasn't very cold. There was lots of sun, and there wasn't any wind. It was a good day for _____.

   a. walking in the park
   b. talking on the phone
   c. working in the office
   d. watching television

5. Last night we went to a café. A band was playing jazz music. But we didn't have a nice evening. The band was terrible, and the _____.

   a. people were friendly
   b. movie was bad
   c. food was good
   d. room was hot

6. There was a dead bird in the yard this morning. Leila saw the bird and started to cry. She was very upset. That was the first time she saw _____.

   a. a dead animal
   b. lots of cars
   c. lots of birds
   d. a dead person

B. *Talk about your answers with another student. Are they the same?*

A. Circle the best answer.

1. Selma is from Istanbul, but now she lives in Toronto. She enjoys her new life. She's an artist. She paints and draws pictures for children's books. She likes her work, and she _____.
   a. doesn't like Toronto   c. likes Istanbul
   b. doesn't like Istanbul   d. likes Toronto

2. Ferrari cars are famous all around the world. People like to look at them in car shows or on television. But most people can't buy them because Ferraris are very _____.
   a. fast   c. expensive
   b. beautiful   d. red

3. Laura lived with her mother for most of her life. She never did any housework. Her mother did it all. Then her mother died. At the age of 60, Laura learned to _____.
   a. cook and clean   c. eat and drink
   b. read and write   d. work and play

4. When Maria was young, she went to work in another city. She felt very lonely and unhappy. But after a few months, she made some friends. She was much happier _____.
   a. after that   c. before that
   b. alone   d. at home

5. The Space Needle is a very tall building in Seattle. There's a restaurant at the top. It's not like other restaurants in Seattle. From your table, you can see _____.
   a. all of the city   c. the kitchen
   b. lots of trees   d. people eating

6. Every year there is a big soccer game between Bologna and Modena. Many people go to the game. This year Modena won. The people from Modena were very happy. They _____.
   a. sat quietly   c. talked on telephones
   b. went home   d. shouted and sang

B. Talk about your answers with another student. Are they the same?

EXERCISE 1

A.   Circle the best answer.

1. Tadek almost always has a sandwich for lunch. Sometimes his sandwich has eggs, and sometimes it has ham. But today he doesn't want a sandwich for lunch. He wants _____.

   a. breakfast
   b. a cheese sandwich
   c. some pizza
   d. to meet friends

2. Michelle and Micol are twin sisters. They look the same, but they are very different. Michelle is very quiet, but Micol likes to talk. Michelle is afraid of new people, but Micol likes _____.

   a. staying alone
   b. reading books
   c. playing with her sister
   d. meeting new people

3. Yoko was very upset yesterday. Something terrible happened in Japan. There was an earthquake. Many buildings fell down, and about 5,000 people died. Many people now have no homes. They are living in _____.

   a. houses
   b. schools
   c. Japan
   d. families

4. In Linda's living room, there are lots of books and paintings. There are plants, a piano, and a telephone. But there is no television. Linda doesn't like _____.

   a. reading books
   b. watching movies
   c. talking on the phone
   d. watching television

5. Susanna and Miguel have an ice-cream shop. They work very long hours in the summer. They work less in the spring and fall. In the winter, they close the shop and _____.

   a. sell lots of ice cream
   b. make ice cream
   c. work very hard
   d. take a vacation

6. Dr. Kapoor gets up at 6:00 A.M. every day and goes to the hospital. In the afternoon, he goes to his office. Then he goes back to the hospital. He often gets home after 9:00 P.M. He has a very long _____.

    a. work day   c. vacation
    b. office hours   d. free time

B. *Talk about your answers with another student. Are they the same?*

EXERCISE 2

A. *Circle the best answer.*

1. We never go to the French restaurants in New York because they're expensive. We like to go to the Chinese restaurants or the Brazilian restaurants. They _____.
    a. don't cost as much   c. aren't very good
    b. cost a lot of money   d. are hard to find

2. John and Shonni often go to a Brazilian restaurant where there's music. A Brazilian band plays the music, and the people in the restaurant sometimes start dancing. John and Shonni _____.
    a. don't like dancing   c. like music and dancing
    b. like Brazilian coffee   d. like Scottish dancing

3. Paula is the new manager of a big company. At first, the workers didn't want a woman manager, but now they like her a lot. She's a very friendly person, and she always _____.
    a. walks away   c. talks on the phone
    b. listens to them   d. works late

4. At 3:45 P.M., Marta stops working. She puts on her coat and leaves the office. She drives for ten minutes to her son's school. She arrives just when the children _____.
    a. go in   c. run away
    b. get out   d. come home

5. Bruce Wilson worked for the Acme paper company for 40 years. Then, last year, he stopped working. The people at the company were sad when he stopped. Bruce was a good worker and a _____.
    a. difficult person   c. nice person
    b. better man   d. older man

6. Many people talk to their computers. When the computer works slowly, they tell it to go faster. When it doesn't work at all, they shout at it. They forget that a computer is _____.

    a. always on   c. usually fast

    b. a machine   d. like a person

B. *Talk about your answers with another student. Are they the same?*

EXERCISE 3

A. *Circle the best answer.*

    1. Last year my friend Kiri went to Korea. She wanted to learn about the country and write some newspaper stories about it. But she had one big problem. She couldn't talk to people because she _____.

        a. didn't like Korean food   c. couldn't speak English

        b. couldn't speak Korean   d. didn't have a newspaper

    2. Saffa was afraid of mice. One day she saw a mouse in the kitchen. She jumped onto a chair and shouted for her mother. Her mother came and caught the mouse. Then Saffa _____.

        a. got off the chair   c. jumped onto the table

        b. went under the table   d. shouted at her mother

    3. Many young girls like dancing and want to be famous dancers. They think that dancers are beautiful, and that dancing is fun. But dancers don't always have fun. They often have _____.

        a. long legs   c. an easy life

        b. a lot of money   d. many difficulties

    4. My cat likes to sit on my car. It's her favorite place. From there she can see all the people on the street. She can also see all the dogs. The dogs can see her, but they can't _____.

        a. catch her   c. smell her

        b. hear her   d. look at her

    5. Akira was the only child from Japan in his class. There were some children from Russia, Israel, China, and Korea. There were lots of Mexicans and Salvadorans. But there were no other _____.

        a. American children   c. small children

        b. Korean children   d. Japanese children

6. This morning I talked with Mr. Swenson. He told me the town wants to build a new road. They want to build it through his yard. He's very angry because he doesn't want _____.
   a. a road in his yard
   b. a new yard
   c. more roads in town
   d. buildings in his yard

B. *Talk about your answers with another student. Are they the same?*

EXERCISE 4

A. *Circle the best answer.*

1. Something happened to the computer in the office yesterday morning. It stopped working, and we couldn't start it again. In the afternoon, we had to do all our work _____.
   a. with it
   b. outside
   c. without it
   d. together

2. The new boy had many problems at school. The other children didn't like him, and the teachers were always angry with him. He told his parents, but they didn't _____.
   a. look at him
   b. listen to him
   c. teach him
   d. wake him

3. Dick makes lots of phone calls. He talks with his brother in Mumbai and with his friends in Berlin, Singapore, and Mexico City. He used to spend a lot on his phone calls. But now he uses his computer to call and he _____.
   a. spends even more
   b. can hear better
   c. spends much less
   d. waits for their calls

4. Judd has some big news. The family is going to move to another city soon. He and his wife are going to start new jobs. The children are going to _____.
   a. go to new schools
   b. see old friends
   c. start new jobs
   d. learn new languages

5. Here's your sandwich and some fruit juice. Now take your bicycle and go! You don't want to be late for work. You were late yesterday and the day before. Go fast and _____!
   a. stop often
   b. go home
   c. say hello
   d. don't stop

6. Look at all the cars. We can't get off this road, and we can't go on any other road. We have to sit here and wait. The CD player doesn't work, so we can't even _____.

    a. get out of the car   c. listen to music

    b. go home today   d. read the newspaper

B. **Talk about your answers with another student. Are they the same?**

EXERCISE 5

A. **Circle the best answer.**

1. Lin lives in New York City. Sometimes she sees famous people near her home. She tells her family. Her family lives in Iowa, and they don't see many famous people. Not as many famous people

    _____.

    a. go to New York   c. live in Iowa

    b. go to work   d. have friends

2. Look at that woman! All the people on the street are looking at her. She's young and very beautiful. She has very nice, expensive clothes. Now some people are taking pictures of her. I think she's famous. _____?

    a. Who are they   c. What is it

    b. Where is she   d. Who is she

3. Marvin liked going for bike rides with his friends. He often went out with them in the morning and came back many hours later. They all rode very fast on their bicycles. In a short time, they could ride

    _____.

    a. a few minutes   c. many miles

    b. another way   d. to work

4. There was a letter on my desk. Now it's not there! Do you know where it is? It's a very important letter from the bank. I have to answer it soon. But I can't answer it if I can't _____.

    a. learn it   c. lose it

    b. find it   d. send it

5. Jorge's parents have a Mexican restaurant in Washington, D.C. It's right in the center of the city, and it's a very popular place. Many important people in the government eat there. One time the American president _____.

    a. ate lunch at home   c. had dinner there
    b. was in Washington   d. went to a restaurant

6. Many famous people were at the party in New York City. There was the president of a big company and the president of a big university. A famous doctor was there and a famous writer. There were also _____.

    a. some movie stars   c. old friends from school
    b. lots of drinks   d. parties in other places

B. **Talk about your answers with another student. Are they the same?**

EXERCISE 6

A. **Circle the best answer.**

1. Shirin and Azra wanted to visit their teacher in the hospital. She had to have an operation last week, and she's still there. But the doctor told them it was not a good day for a visit. He told them to try again _____.

    a. yesterday   c. at school
    b. another day   d. in an hour

2. Frank had an important meeting yesterday. He talked to the new manager of the company. The manager told Frank some good news. He wants Frank to change jobs. His new job will not be easy, but Frank will _____.

    a. make more money   c. work long hours
    b. have no money   d. do his old job

3. Yesterday we went to see a great movie. It was about a man named Jack. He loves a woman named Jill. But Jill loves a man named Jarvis. Jarvis loves Janet, and Janet loves Jack. It was very funny, and of course, it _____.

    a. had a terrible ending   c. was not very interesting
    b. was in black and white   d. had a happy ending

4. Some people eat too many sweets. Their favorite foods are sweets. They eat lots of cookies, candy, and ice cream. They don't eat many fruits or vegetables. These people may get sick one day. Sweets are not _____.

    a. very expensive   c. fun to eat

    b. hard to find   d. good for you

5. Yesterday morning my refrigerator was empty. I had no money, so I went to the bank machine on the way to work. But the bank machine wasn't working, so I couldn't buy any breakfast. By 11:00 A.M., I _____.

    a. didn't want to eat   c. was very hungry

    b. was very tired   d. had a lot of money

6. Zoe looked at her apartment. It was terrible! There were bottles and glasses on all the tables. There was food on the sofa and on the floor. She said to her son, "I'm going out for a few minutes. When I come back, I don't want to _____!"

    a. see these things   c. see this place

    b. eat any food   d. have a party

B. **Talk about your answers with another student. Are they the same?**

EXERCISE 7

A. **Circle the best answer.**

1. Sonia met an interesting young man at the party last night. She told me all about him. He's tall and good-looking. He has a very interesting job, and he likes to travel. He's not married, and he doesn't have a girlfriend. I think Sonia _____.

    a. doesn't like him at all   c. likes another man

    b. wants to see him again   d. is going to a party

2. This is not a good place to live. The weather is terrible. In the summer, it's too hot, and it doesn't rain for months. In the winter, it's very cold, and it rains all the time. It's nice here only _____.

    a. in spring and fall   c. in the evening hours

    b. on long weekends   d. in the summer months

3. In 1994 Wanda opened a new store. She sold children's clothing. It was not easy at first, and she had many problems. But after a few years, business was good at the store. Many people in town bought clothes _____.

   a. from friends   c. at Wanda's store
   b. in big stores   d. at the market

4. Rhonda doesn't like the winter in England. She doesn't like cold weather, and she doesn't like short days. She wants to live in a place with warm winters. She says she's going to sell her house and _____.

   a. build a new one   c. go live in Russia
   b. start a business   d. move to Spain

5. Coffee was Ronald's favorite drink. He drank four or five cups of coffee a day. Then the doctor told him to stop drinking coffee. Ronald didn't know what to drink. He didn't want to drink tea. He said, "Only sick people _____."

   a. drink tea   c. go to the doctor
   b. like coffee   d. have breakfast

6. The English homework for tomorrow is very easy. We have to read one page of our book and do some exercises in the workbook. I can do it all tomorrow before class. This evening I don't want to do homework. I want to have fun and _____.

   a. do Spanish homework   c. write an English paper
   b. go out with my friends d. speak lots of English

B. *Talk about your answers with another student. Are they the same?*

EXERCISE 8

A. *Circle the best answer.*

1. Do you have to go now? Why don't you stay for dinner? I can make a very nice meal for us. Do you like fish? I have fish and vegetables and rice. I also have some wine and some ice cream. Please don't go. I can't eat _____!

   a. an early dinner   c. meat and potatoes
   b. lots of ice cream   d. all this food alone

(continued)

2. There's no train to our small town, and there are only a few buses. Everyone uses cars. During the week, they drive to work in the city and home again. On the weekends, the city people drive here to the country. There are always a lot of cars _____.

   a. in the city   c. on our roads
   b. at our house   d. on Mondays

3. Last summer we went to the mountains for our vacation. We stayed in a beautiful place, and the people were very nice. But it rained every afternoon! We don't want to go back to the mountains this summer. We want to go to _____.

   a. the supermarket   c. work all summer
   b. the seaside   d. the mountains again

4. The manager at work is angry with John. She says he comes in too late and goes home too early. He should be at work by 9:00 A.M., and he should stay until 5:00 P.M. But often he arrives at 9:15 and goes home _____.

   a. before 5:00 P.M.   c. at 5:15 P.M.
   b. very late   d. for lunch

5. Did you see the movie on television last night? It was a very sad movie about World War II. There was a little Jewish boy named Jonah from Holland. Those were terrible times for Jewish people. The Nazis in Germany killed millions of Jews. Jonah lived, but _____.

   a. his mother lived, too   c. his parents died
   b. the Germans died   d. he didn't die

6. Friday was the last day of the English course. There was a party in the evening, and all the students came. They had food and drinks, a CD player, and lots of CDs. Some students talked, and others danced. They all had a good time, and they didn't _____.

   a. want to go home   c. stay for long
   b. like the party   d. say anything

B. Talk about your answers with another student. Are they the same?

Credits

Text Credits: Page 161 excerpt from *Mike's Lucky Day*, by Leslie Dunkling, © 2008 Penguin Readers published by Pearson Education Limited; **Page 162** excerpt from *The Battle of Newton Road*, by Leslie Dunkling, © 2008 Penguin Readers published by Pearson Education Limited; **Page 163** excerpt from *Tinker's Farm* by Stephen Rabley, © 1990 Penguin Readers published by Pearson Education Limited; **Page 164** excerpt from *Island for Sale* by Anne Collins, © 1992 Penguin Readers published by Pearson Education Limited. www.penguinreaders.com. Reprinted with permission.

Photo Credits: Part 1 Opener © iStockphoto.com; **Page 3** © Corbis Yellow RF; **Page 29** © Shutterstock; **Page 33** © iStockphoto.com; **Page 37** © AP Images; **Page 41** © Envision/Corbis; **Page 49** from *The Big Bag Mistake*, © 1992 Penguin Readers published by Pearson Education Limited; **Part 2 Opener** © Shutterstock; **Page 75** © Shutterstock; **Part 3 Opener** © Shutterstock; **Page 145** © David Baker/Alamy; **Page 147** © Robert Harding/Corbis; **Page 154** © Yellow Dog Productions/Getty Images; **Part 4 Opener** © Shutterstock